Mormonism: A Very Short Introduction

VERY SHORT INTRODUCTIONS are for anyone wanting a stimulating and accessible way in to a new subject. They are written by experts, and have been published in more than 25 languages worldwide.

The series began in 1995, and now represents a wide variety of topics in history, philosophy, religion, science, and the humanities. Over the next few years it will grow to a library of around 200 volumes — a Very Short Introduction to everything from ancient Egypt and Indian philosophy to conceptual art and cosmology.

Very Short Introductions available now:

Available soon:

For more information visit our web site
www.oup.co.uk/general/vsi/

Richard Lyman Bushman

MORMONISM

A Very Short Introduction

OXFORD
UNIVERSITY PRESS

OXFORD
UNIVERSITY PRESS

Oxford University Press, Inc., publishes works that
further Oxford University's objective of excellence
in research, scholarship, and education.

Oxford New York
Auckland Cape Town Dar es Salaam Hong Kong Karachi
Kuala Lumpur Madrid Melbourne Mexico City Nairobi
New Delhi Shanghai Taipei Toronto

With offices in
Argentina Austria Brazil Chile Czech Republic France Greece
Guatemala Hungary Italy Japan Poland Portugal Singapore
South Korea Switzerland Thailand Turkey Ukraine Vietnam

Copyright © 2008 by Richard Lyman Bushman

Published by Oxford University Press, Inc.
198 Madison Avenue, New York, NY 10016

www.oup.com

Oxford is a registered trademark of Oxford University Press

Library of Congress Cataloging-in-Publication Data
Bushman, Richard L.
Mormonism : a very short introduction / Richard Lyman Bushman.
p. cm.— (Very short introductions)
Includes bibliographical references and index.
ISBN 978-0-19-531030-6 (pbk.)
1. Church of Jesus Christ of Latter-day Saints.
2. Mormon Church. I. Title.
BX8635.3.B87 2008
289.3—dc22
2007044444

7 9 8 6

Printed in Great Britain by
Ashford Colour Press Ltd, Gosport, Hants.
on acid-free paper

For Jed Woodworth
Comrade and Friend

Contents

List of illustrations

Illustrations courtesy of Church History Library, Church of Jesus Christ
of Latter-day Saints.

Preface

Mormonism has intrigued readers ever since Joseph Smith first published the Book of Mormon in Palmyra, New York, in 1830. Scarcely a year later, the newspaper reporter James Gordon Bennett filed an article with the *New York Morning Enquirer and Courier* with the opening line: "You have heard of Mormonism—who has not?" Smith's extraordinary claims to revelations immediately made Mormonism good press. Visionaries were common in that period, but not ones who published volumes of newly translated ancient scripture.

Interest in Mormonism did not flag during Joseph Smith's life, and in the second half of the nineteenth century, Brigham Young's settlement of the Great Basin of the western United States and the practice of polygamy kept the nation's attention focused on Utah. Between the moral outrage against plural marriage and the titillation of lurid stories of Mormon excess, Mormonism was constantly in the news.

Not until the twentieth century did the coverage turn away from the sensational to Mormons' social virtues. By the mid-twentieth century, Mormons were known for their strong families and communal cooperation. The organization of the welfare program to provide for Mormon poor during the Depression and the radio broadcasts of the Mormon Tabernacle Choir from Temple Square in Salt Lake City gave Mormonism an attractive face.

But if the Mormon people are better appreciated now than a century ago, the Mormon religion still baffles outsiders. How can twenty-first-century Americans believe in a prophet who translated gold plates and claimed constant revelations? The emergence of eminent Mormon politicians, business leaders, and entertainers only deepens the mystery. Sane, useful, upright members of society hold beliefs that others find difficult to understand, much less believe. The jarring contradiction leads to a question: Why does Mormonism exercise such a powerful influence on the lives of Mormons? How can a religion that runs against the grain of modern secularism evoke such strong loyalties? This book tries to answer this question.

Richard Bushman
Pasadena, California
August 2007

Chapter 1
Introduction

The religious movement known as Mormonism began with the visions of Joseph Smith in upstate New York around 1820. In 1830, Smith organized a church with a tiny handful of members. Today the largest body of Mormons, known officially as the Church of Jesus Christ of Latter-day Saints (LDS), has nearly thirteen million members, more than half of them outside the United States. A smaller group, once known as the Reorganized Church of Jesus Christ of Latter Day Saints (RLDS) and now as the Community of Christ, has a membership of about 250,000 in fifty countries.

From its headquarters in Salt Lake City, the Church of Jesus Christ of Latter-day Saints directs a worldwide missionary force of more than fifty thousand young men and women readily identifiable by their conservative dress and name tags. Although its adherents regard it as a restoration of ancient Christianity, Mormonism holds a number of distinctive doctrines and practices, among them belief in a scripture supplemental to the Bible known as the Book of Mormon, the source of the movement's nickname.

For many people, the mention of Mormons conjures up an assortment of contradictory images. Fresh-faced missionaries knocking on doors with a religious message; the Mormon Tabernacle Choir broadcasting on Sunday mornings from Temple

Square in Salt Lake City; church members cooperating to provide for their own poor; Brigham Young University students consistently being voted the most strait-laced college students in the United States; tightly knit families teaching their children to live clean lives: All these suggest that Mormons are happy, uncomplicated, kindly, and innocent—if perhaps naïve.

A contrasting set of associations begins with the extravagant stories of the founder of Mormonism, Joseph Smith. Smith claimed that an angel directed him to gold plates, which he translated as the Book of Mormon. In the 1840s, he instituted plural marriage among his followers, and in 1844, he was assassinated by his non-Mormon enemies. His successor, Brigham Young, took scores of wives after he led the Mormons to Utah in 1847. Today, some people think of a powerful religious hierarchy controlling the church from the top. These less innocent Mormons are secretive, clannish, and perhaps dangerous. Frequently Mormonism is labeled a cult rather than a church. Some say it is not Christian.

Which of these is the true Mormonism? Are both descriptions accurate? Mormons react strongly to the negative images of themselves. They wholeheartedly believe the stories of Joseph Smith and the gold plates. The visit of the angel and the translation of the Book of Mormon, far from being fabulous fairy tales, constitute Mormonism's founding miracles, the equivalent of the resurrection of Jesus for traditional Christians or the deliverance of Israel from Egypt for the Jews. Yes, these are controversial, Mormons say, but founding miracles always are. Miracles give a religion its original impetus, its evidence that God intervenes in human life, while at the same time they are its most contested assertions. The resurrection of Jesus is fiercely debated to this day.

The polygamy charge annoys Mormons because it is so far out of date. The largest body of the Mormons, the Church of Jesus Christ of Latter-day Saints, renounced polygamy in 1890 and officially forbids the practice. The church has not repudiated the plural marriages of nineteenth-century Mormons, but they are long past. Mormons point out that God commanded Abraham, Isaac, and Jacob to practice polygamy at the foundation of Israel; plural marriage served the same purpose when the Mormon people were coming into existence. Now the church is entirely monogamous and emphasizes fidelity between husband and wife as strongly as any religion in the world.

As for the church hierarchy, Mormons honor church leaders just as early Christians honored Peter and Paul. A central principle of Mormonism is belief in ongoing revelation. The prophets and apostles who head the church, Mormons believe, receive revelation for the management of church affairs as did prophets and apostles in the Bible. Church members like the idea of being led by revelation. Some complain about the "counsel" of church leaders, but most happily receive the directions of the prophet-president of the church as the will of the Lord for our time.

Mormons turn many of the common negative images into positives, but others they reject. They deny the assertion that Mormonism is a cult. How can a church with nearly thirteen million members, scattered all over the world, be considered a cult? By sociological definition, one key feature of a cult is high tension with the surrounding society. Yet Mormons blend with society. They seek political office, rise to high places in business corporations, work as musicians and artists, seek education in eminent graduate schools, and teach in universities. Today, more than a century and three-quarters since its organization in 1830, Mormonism feels more like a church than a cult.

The charge that Mormons are not Christians puzzles Latter-day Saints more than any other criticism. Does not the name of the church convey devotion to Christ? Mormons believe Christ is the divine Son of God who died for humanity's sins, was resurrected, and sits on the right hand of God. Mormons pray in the name of

Christ, covenant weekly to remember him always, and strive to keep his commandments. What more should they do? The answer, of course, is that they should accept the traditional interpretation of the Bible as embodied in the creeds of Christendom, and this Mormons do not do. Mormons would say they are biblical Christians but not creedal Christians.

Restoration

Mormons speak of their entire movement as the restoration. The doctrines they teach are called the restored gospel. The word implies that something essential was lost from the Christian churches and had to be brought back. The words *Latter-day Saints* in the church's name refer implicitly to the "saints" of former days when Christ called his disciples. Mormons think of themselves as "Saints" of the latter days, renewing the mission begun by Christ and his apostles at the beginning of the Christian era.

The word *restoration* was not original with Mormons. They borrowed the term from Walter Scott, a Reformed Baptist preacher working in northeast Ohio where the Mormons settled. "Restored" refers to the restoration of biblical Christianity from the distortions and accretions that were thought to have accumulated over the centuries under Roman Catholicism. "Restoration" in the broadest sense underlay the work of reformers from Martin Luther on. The reformers strove to recover the authentic faith of Paul's Christianity. The Puritans thought of themselves as restorers of the primitive church.

Joseph Smith's restoration, however, took a slightly different turn. For most restorationists, the Bible offered a blueprint for constructing true religion. They set up the scriptures as a standard of Christian worship and tried to conform their belief and practices to its pattern. Joseph Smith used the term *restoration* but went about his work differently. His contemporary and rival, the restorationist Alexander Campbell, founder of the Disciples of

Christ, brought years of thought to bear on his interpretation of the Bible. His restoration came out of intensive study and discussion. Smith's teachings did not come through training and study at all. He had little education and rarely attended church as a boy. Joseph Smith's interpretation came from what he called "marvilous experience."[1] He did not analyze the Bible and derive his doctrines from its pages; he learned from his own revelations. He claimed, in other words, to write and interpret scripture as the original biblical prophets did.

Campbell's followers thought Smith carried restorationism too far. The Campbellites hewed closely to New Testament doctrine, church organization, and worship, but they did not claim revelation or apostolic authority. Joseph Smith restored not only the forms of New Testament religion but its power. He claimed revelation like Peter and Paul, wrote scripture, and claimed direct authority from God. Angels visited him and bestowed their powers. Rather than emulating biblical religion, the Mormons in their own eyes reenacted it.

All forms of restorationism give their adherents a sense of history, but Smith's way of reading history differed from the rest. He did not think of himself as going back to a primordium of true Christianity, as the Puritans did. In his view, there never was a golden age when religion flourished to perfection. Smith saw himself as completing a work that had never been perfectly realized. Beginning with Adam, God had pursued his purposes through the ages, working through the prophets to create a righteous people, but that work had always been thwarted; the prophets were killed, and the people lapsed into apostasy. Now, in the closing times of the earth's history, the kingdom of God was at last to be established. All the powers and knowledge of earlier ages were to be restored to bring God's plans for the earth to completion prior to the Second Coming of Christ. Visitors from past eras of sacred history—Elijah, John the Baptist, Peter—bestowed the knowledge and authority that would equip the modern church to finish the work. The early Latter-day Saints felt they were living at the culminating point in world history. Indeed, the term *latter-day* refers to their sense of living in the last days of the earth.

Although one purpose of restoration was to identify the errors in traditional Christianity, Smith did not enter into debates with Christian theologians or overtly contest the creeds. He was not a controversialist. He simply announced new doctrines rather than posing them against the errors in traditional Christian belief. He pictured his revelations as a flood of knowledge pouring from heaven like a refreshing rain. The outcome, however, was no less radical. One of the most telling was a reconceptualization of God.

Early passages in Smith's revelations could be interpreted as traditionally trinitarian, but the doctrine of three Gods in one soon gave way to a Father, Son, and Holy Ghost, three distinct beings united in purpose and will but not in substance. Christ, in other words, was not a manifestation of the one and only God, but a separate being altogether. Mormons believe in what is sometimes called "social trinitarianism," meaning the three beings of the Godhead are blended in heart and mind like extremely close friends but are not one being. Even more radically, Smith declared that the Father and the Son were persons with human forms. "The Father has a body of flesh and bones as tangible as man's," Smith stated bluntly, "the Son also; but the Holy Ghost has not a body of flesh and bones, but is a personage of Spirit" (Doctrine and Covenants 130:22).

The idea of a corporeal God was not unknown in Smith's time. It was probably how most ordinary Christians thought about God—as a person in a human form. Religious art had always pictured God in a body, and the visionaries of Joseph Smith's time saw him in the form of a man. To uninitiated readers of the Bible, the obvious meaning of Genesis 1:26, "let us make man in our own image, after our own likeness," was that God had a human shape. The same was true for the occasion when Moses spoke with God "face to face" (Exodus 33:11). The incarnation of Jesus seemed to prove that God could take the form of a man, and the resurrection showed he could continue in human form in heaven. If Jesus is the revelation of God, then God is a man.

For centuries, theologians in the church had struggled to reconcile the humanity of Jesus—his immanence—and the utter transcendence of God. In Joseph Smith's time, unlike two centuries earlier in the Puritan era, ordinary Christians leaned toward Jesus' humanity. The loving Jesus was the God who redeemed them in conversion. The transcendent God of Calvinism was beyond their ken. In Calvinist doctrine, God is an entirely different order of being. Nothing affects him—no suffering, no evil, no goodness. He cannot be said to have form or feeling. He is what he is and does as he wills. Theologically speaking, he exists outside of time and space, outside of the realm of human understanding, outside of all known forms of existence.

Most Christian theologians held on to both transcendence and immanence in their doctrine of God. Smith came down entirely on the side of immanence. Perhaps his single greatest theological departure was to state that God was of the same order of being as humans. Smith would not have used that formal language, but his description of God's body of flesh and bone amounted to the same thing. God's transcendence took the form of his might, glory, holiness, and intelligence. But, though exalted and powerful beyond our comprehension, God has the form and substance of a man. We humans exist in the same ontological realm as the creator of heaven and earth. We are even of the same species.

That "collapse of sacred distance," as one Mormon theologian has called it, gives Mormonism its distinctive flavor. Brigham Young said Joseph Smith made heaven and earth shake hands. Mormons feel that God is accessible to them; he is their father and they his children. They can even aspire, with his encouragement and direction, to become like him. The Mormon God is immanent not only in the incarnation of Jesus but in his own being as a person of flesh and bone like his earthly children. He has a body just as we do, making bodies not a fleshly burden and curse but a source of joy and exaltation.

Mormons think that Christianity's belief in a God outside of time and space infiltrated into traditional Christian teachings from Greek philosophy. The learning of men had obscured the plain meaning of the Bible. Smith's calling was to restore what was lost.

Joseph Smith Jr.

The role of Joseph Smith in Mormonism is difficult to keep in focus. He was the church's first prophet and the founder of the faith, but he is not preeminent. As the formal name of the church, the Church of Jesus Christ of Latter-day Saints, suggests, Jesus Christ is the premier figure. Smith does not even play the role of the last and culminating prophet, as Muhammad does in Islam. In the Mormon view, many prophets preceded Smith and many will follow. Nor is he a model of virtuous conduct like Muhammad. Smith warned his followers not to idolize him, insisting on his own human failings.

But for Mormons, he is nonetheless the prophet of the restoration, the man to return Christianity to its own true nature. Because he played a leading role in this era of world history, his life figures prominently in the Mormon imagination. Mormons wonder how a person of such modest capacities was able to write the Book of Mormon, organize a church, and propound so much intriguing doctrine. Smith's rudimentary education barely enabled him to read and write; he had read little more than the Bible before his emergence as a church leader. How did he so naturally form a church and gather his followers into a holy city? By age twenty-four, he had published the Book of Mormon, a 584-page book of prophecy, history, and revelation, had organized a church, and was presuming to correct the Bible. Whence this immense confidence?

Smith was born December 23, 1805, in Sharon, Vermont. He was the fifth-generation descendant of English ancestors who came to Massachusetts in the Puritan migration of the 1630s. The Smiths lived in Topsfield, just west of Salem, Massachusetts, until Asael Smith, Joseph's grandfather, moved from Massachusetts to Vermont in the 1790s in search of land for his family of boys. His son Joseph Smith Sr. lost his farm when he overextended himself in ill-starred business ventures and in 1816 moved with his family to Palmyra, New York, along the route of the future Erie Canal. There he purchased another farm but eventually lost it to creditors. In 1830, when Joseph Smith Jr. organized the church, his fifty-eight-year-old father was landless. Like those of thousands of other farmers in his time, Joseph Sr.'s fortunes followed a downward as well as a westward trajectory.

In moving from New England, the Smiths also lost touch with the Congregational Church inherited from their Puritan ancestors. Joseph Smith Sr. lapsed into a disconsolate skepticism about churches. He yearned for salvation without knowing where to turn. His children were reared without a church. When late in life his wife, Lucy Smith, joined the Presbyterian Church in Palmyra, Joseph Sr. and Joseph Jr. stayed home.

In the Smiths' Palmyra, however, the question of how to be saved could not be avoided. The town stood in the path of the ongoing campaign to save souls that was later called the Second Great Awakening. Evangelical pastors pressed the question of salvation at their weekly meetings, and itinerant preachers stirred the population in periodic camp meeting revivals. Joseph Smith later said that he wanted to "feel & shout like the Rest but could feel nothing."[2] With little guidance from his parents and lacking a family pastor, he was thrown back on his own resources.

Around 1820, when he was fourteen, Smith began to receive the revelations that started him on his course as a prophet. Ten years later, on April 6, 1830, he organized the church first known as the

9

Church of Christ. For the next fourteen years, Smith headed the church as First Elder and later as president. Followers came to him through personal friends and family connections, and then by active proselytizing after Smith ordained virtually every male convert as a missionary. Going out whenever circumstances allowed, this corps of teachers spread across the northeastern United States and later the whole country with news of a new revelation and the restoration of the ancient religion. Proselytizing in Europe began in 1837. Membership grew steadily to probably more than twenty-five thousand by the time of Smith's death in 1844, with a significant part of the church by then located in Great Britain.

Shortly after the church's organization in 1830, missionaries made more than a hundred converts in northeast Ohio, prompting Smith to move his headquarters from New York to Kirtland, near Cleveland, in 1831. At the same time, his revelations instructed him to locate a site for a City of Zion where converts were to gather in preparation for the Second Coming of Christ. In a time of high millennial excitement, the idea of a place of refuge in the coming calamities was appealing. Smith chose the village of Independence in Jackson County, Missouri, at the far edge of American settlement, and directed members to gather there as well as in Kirtland. (Independence would later be known as the hometown of U.S. president Harry Truman, and Jackson County for its largest city, Kansas City, Missouri.)

For the remainder of his life, Smith focused on building the City of Zion with a social order devoted to equality and unity. Zion was Smith's favorite topic, one of his clerks wrote. He perpetually hoped that next year his people would be living together in Zion. But his dreams would not be fulfilled. His plans were repeatedly thwarted by the opposition that arose wherever the Mormons settled. Established residents tolerated a handful of religious eccentrics in their communities; they became alarmed when the strange religionists threatened to become a majority. Unable to expel the Mormons legally, the citizens resorted to vigilante action. In Jackson County, they ordered the Mormons to leave and backed up their demands with tar and feathers, whippings, and crop-burnings.

Mormons were driven from Independence in the fall of 1833, moving eventually into unoccupied areas of northern Missouri, where they established another gathering place at Far West. Wherever they settled, however, animosity built up. In 1838, the state government forced the Mormons to leave Missouri altogether. Joseph Smith was arrested and held in a damp, cold prison for six months. In the meantime, the Mormons fled east across the Mississippi River to Illinois and founded another city. After escaping his captors (probably with their collusion), Smith joined his people and named the new city Nauvoo, a Hebrew word he interpreted to mean "beautiful place."

In Nauvoo, Smith came closest to building the city he had long dreamed of. Converts flowed in from all over the United States and after 1841 from Great Britain. Although it was primarily a "city of Saints," as the Mormons called themselves because of the church's name, the Nauvoo City Council passed a toleration act to welcome people of all religions. Blithely merging church and state, Smith was elected mayor and lieutenant general of the local militia. Before he died, Nauvoo had five thousand residents, as many as Chicago, with the same number or more in the surrounding countryside.

Instead of bringing peace, however, prosperity once more triggered anger and fear. In addition to the usual opposition from the non-Mormon citizenry, dissent rose within the Mormon ranks. Smith's institution of plural marriage among thirty or so of his closest associates, though practiced secretly, appalled others who learned of it. A handful of them organized a reform church within Nauvoo and invited disaffected Mormons to join. Outside the city,

1. **A sketch of Joseph Smith by Sutcliffe Maudsley, 1843.**

anti-Mormon rage rose to fever pitch. Nearby editors called for the expulsion of the Mormons and threatened Smith's life. When the Mormon dissenters published a protest paper, the *Nauvoo Expositor*, in May 1844, the city council, fearing it would spark another attack from the Mormons' outside antagonists, closed the paper.

This infringement on press rights ignited a conflagration. The local population interpreted the closing of the press as an intolerable instance of Mormon fanaticism. Joseph Smith was carried to the county seat for trial. On June 27, 1844, a mob stormed his prison cell in Carthage and shot him to death.

The citizens of the county expected a Mormon uprising to avenge the death of their prophet, but the Mormons, recognizing their vulnerable position, kept the peace. In August they chose Brigham Young as their new leader. Young claimed the position not as a prophet in his own right but as the senior member of the Quorum of the Twelve Apostles, the leading council of the church under Joseph Smith. Young hoped the death of the Mormon prophet would calm the opposition, but in the fall of 1845, the Illinois government asked the Mormons to leave in order to forestall a violent onslaught. Forced to depart in the winter cold, the first body of Mormons crossed the Mississippi River in February 1846, eventually embarking on their famous trek west to what was to become the state of Utah.

Mormonism thus began in an efflorescence of revelation and violence. Killed at age thirty-eight after fourteen years as head of the church, Smith left his followers the Book of Mormon, a book of his own revelations called the Doctrine and Covenants, an organization led by Apostles, and a conviction that Mormons possessed the restored gospel of Christ. Over the years, Mormonism passed through one dramatic transition after another, but Smith's influence never faded. He did not recede into a dim past as the followers who had known him personally died. He remains a vivid presence in the Mormon religious imagination to this day, his writings and thought shaping Mormon religious life as definitively now as ever.

Varieties of Mormonism

Mormonism now consists of scores of independent factions that have emerged over the years. The church bearing the name of the Church of Jesus Christ of Latter-day Saints, headquartered in Salt

Lake City, Utah, is only the largest entity in a broad movement. A number of separate groups sprang up in the decades after Joseph Smith's death in 1844 when there was a contest to succeed him as president of the church. After Brigham Young led the largest contingent west to the Great Basin in 1847, a substantial number of Mormons who stayed behind formed the Reorganized Church of Jesus Christ of Latter Day Saints under Joseph Smith's son. Known since 2001 as the Community of Christ, this branch of Mormonism is headquartered in Independence, Missouri.

In the early twentieth century, another major split took place following the abandonment of plural marriage in 1890. So-called fundamentalist groups held on to polygamy and claimed to continue authentic Mormonism. They believed that the main body of the church had strayed. The fundamentalists are the groups now notorious in the press for their practice of plural marriage in opposition to anti-bigamy laws.

These divergent wings of the Mormon movement exemplify the complex forces operating within Mormonism to this day. The Community of Christ has taken the course that modernism would seem to dictate. As the Reorganized Church in the nineteenth century, it repudiated the plural marriage of the Utah church. In the twentieth century, the RLDS ordained women while the LDS Church held to its all-male priesthood. In comparison with the Utah-based church, the Community of Christ plays down Joseph Smith, the Book of Mormon, and the miraculous origins. From a modern perspective, it is the "sensible" version of Mormonism, resembling in many respects a liberal Protestant denomination.

The fundamentalist groups, on the other hand, have held on to Mormon extremes. They did not give up plural marriage at the end of the nineteenth century, and some still follow communal economic practices in the manner of the early Mormons. Some of the groups are run by powerful, unchecked male prophets. They seem to live up to the fanatic, anti-modern image of isolated Mormonism.

14

The church headquartered in Salt Lake City is positioned between the two extremes. This book concentrates on the religious life of the Utah-based church because it vastly overshadows the two wings in numbers, but it is also interesting for having synthesized the traditional and the progressive. As it has expanded throughout the world, its members have blended into modern society, all the while keeping the church's miraculous origins at the center of belief.

Mormonism today presents the perplexing contradiction of a miracle-based religion founded in the age of the printing press surviving the onslaught of modern skepticism. Outside observers sometimes react to Mormonism as "nice people, wacky beliefs." Mormons insist that the "wacky" beliefs pull them together as a people and give them the strength and the know-how to succeed in the modern world. The beliefs are partly a theology but just as much a sense of history. Mormons believe that God has again entered history to renew his work. They say that God has called a prophet to prepare for the coming of Christ. Their convictions about what has happened and is happening are as important as their doctrine.

A century and a half after Smith's death, the church still thinks of itself as continuing the work he began. Mormons remain devoutly loyal to their colorful founding prophet. To this day, his varied revelations profoundly shape Mormon life. Viewing modern Mormonism through the prism of Joseph Smith's restoration shows how closely connected they are. A clear line can be traced between each of the major aspects of Smith's teachings—revelation, Zion, priesthood, and cosmology—and the lived religion of Latter-day Saints today.

Chapter 2
Revelation

The First Vision

Joseph Smith's First Vision is now considered to be Mormonism's founding event. Smith said he saw the vision around 1820, when he was about fourteen. He recorded the experience in two main accounts, one in 1832, when he was twenty-six, and the other six years later, in 1838. The two accounts differ in a number of respects. The first is a rough, compressed story with misspelled words and run-on sentences. Written largely in Smith's own hand, the story is fresh and unassuming. The 1838 version is more polished, more suitable for the founding story of the church; it is now appropriately part of Mormon scripture. The 1832 version abbreviates the story of the vision, reporting, for example, that "the Lord" appeared to the young Joseph, whereas the later account speaks of both the Father and the Son.

The two texts have been parsed for their differences, but they clearly tell the same story. In both accounts Smith presents himself as an innocent overcome by his "marvilous experience." In both he begins as a confused boy, concerned for the "wellfare of my immortal soul." As he said in the 1832 version, he was distressed by the failure of Christians to "adorn their profession by a holy walk and Godly conversation."

My mind become excedingly distressed for I become convicted of my sins and by searching the scriptures I found that mankind did not come unto the Lord but that they had apostatised from the true and liveing faith and there was no society or denomination that built upon the gospel of Jesus Christ as recorded in the new testament and I felt to mourn for my own sins and for the sins of the world.[1]

As a young sinner, Smith had nowhere to turn. It seemed to him that the whole world had gone astray.

In desperation, Smith went to a wooded area where his family had been clearing land on their Manchester, New York, farm and prayed for help. He described a "piller of light" coming down from above and the heavens opening to his view.

I saw the Lord and he spake unto me saying Joseph my son thy sins are forgiven thee. go thy way walk in my statutes and keep my commandments.... behold the world lieth in sin at this time and none doeth good no not one they have turned asside from the gospel and keep not my commandments.

The Lord told Smith not to join any of the churches—they were all wrong—and announced that "I come quickly as it is written of me in the cloud clothed in the glory of my Father."[2]

Uncertain what to make of the experience, Smith related his story to a Methodist preacher and was surprised to meet with skepticism. Methodists had been visited with repeated supernatural manifestations for the previous four decades: speaking in tongues, wrenchings of the body by the Holy Spirit, dreams—and visions like Smith's. But as the denomination became more respectable, these extreme behaviors embarrassed the clergy. When Smith told his amazing story, he received the standard reply that miracles had ceased with the apostles. Not understanding Methodism's history, Joseph felt that he had been treated with contempt.

"THIS IS MY BELOVED SON, HEAR HIM!"

2. A stained glass window depiction of Joseph Smith's First Vision, installed in the Adams Ward, Los Angeles, in the early twentieth century.

Rather than doubting his vision, however, Smith lost confidence in the clergy and the churches and chose to live by his own lights. He put his own revelations above the judgment of the learned ministry. In this decision, Mormons see the precedent for the principle governing the church to this day: Every major change in doctrine or policy comes by revelation. Reasoned debate may precede the revelation, but communication from heaven decides the issue, just as it did with Smith at age fourteen. Like all strong founding stories, the First Vision governs and authorizes current practice.

The Book of Mormon

In 1823, about three years after his vision, Joseph Smith prayed to know his standing before the Lord. This time the vision that followed went far beyond the revelations of his contemporaries and even of his own earlier epiphany. Smith said he was visited at night by a brilliant angel later identified as Moroni. The angel assured Smith of forgiveness and told him about golden plates buried in a hill near the Smith farm. On the plates, the angel said, was the history of an ancient people who had been taught the fullness of the gospel of Christ. The next day Smith visited the site, later called the Hill Cumorah, a name assigned in the Book of Mormon, and found the plates in a stone box under a large rock. According to his later account, a supernatural force prevented Smith from obtaining the plates even though they were there in plain sight. For a moment he doubted himself. Had his vision been only a dream? The angel appeared again and told Smith he was stopped in his attempt because his motives were mercenary. He had thought about the value of the gold rather than the history written on the plates and was not yet ready.

The Angel Moroni

After his vision of God and Christ, Joseph Smith said, he fell into many foolish errors and felt the need for forgiveness. On September 21, 1823, when he was seventeen, he prayed in his bedroom to know his standing before the Lord. He later described what happened.

> While I was thus in the act of calling upon God, I discovered a light appearing in my room, which continued to increase until the room was lighter than at noonday, when immediately a personage appeared at my bedside, standing in the air, for his feet did not touch the floor.
>
> He had on a loose robe of most exquisite whiteness. It was a whiteness beyond anything earthly I had ever seen; nor do I believe that any earthly thing could be made to appear so exceedingly white and brilliant. His hands were naked, and his arms also, a little above the wrist; so, also, were his feet naked, as were his legs, a little above the ankles. His head and neck were also bare. I could discover that he had no other clothing on but this robe, as it was open, so that I could see into his bosom.
>
> Not only was his robe exceedingly white, but his whole person was glorious beyond description, and his countenance truly like lightning. The room was exceedingly light, but not so very bright as immediately around his person. When I first looked upon him, I was afraid; but the fear soon left me.
>
> Joseph Smith History, *The Pearl of Great Price* (Salt Lake City: Church of Jesus Christ of Latter-day Saints, 1981), 1:30–32.

It was another four years before Smith actually removed the plates from their box. Meanwhile his family had lost the farm in Manchester and was reduced to tenantry. To help with their finances, Joseph went to work for family friends in southern New York, and while there he renewed his acquaintance with Emma Hale, the daughter of a substantial farmer. Her father forbade them to wed because of Smith's dim prospects, but the young couple was not to be denied. On January 18, 1827, they were married. That fall, on September 22, Joseph obtained the plates and began to translate the ancient record into English with his better-educated wife as scribe.

If Joseph Smith's First Vision came out of a widespread culture of visions, the translation of the Book of Mormon stood out as a singularity. Other people of the time reported seeing Christ; the greatest preacher of the age, Charles G. Finney, said he saw Jesus in the back room of his law office in 1821. But no one but Smith translated a new book of scripture. Young men with ambitions for a religious career customarily followed the well-worn path of preaching. Finney began preaching the day after his vision and did not stop until the end of his life, collecting followers and gaining influence. One acquaintance remarked that as a young man Joseph Smith had been a passable exhorter at a Methodist meeting, meaning that he urged people to comply with the doctrine taught in the more formal sermon, but he is not known to have preached a single sermon to his followers until after the church was organized. Instead he produced a translation of an ancient book.

The translation process is difficult to reconstruct. Purportedly the characters on the golden plates were reformed Egyptian, a form of Hebrew written in Egyptian script. Smith had no knowledge of either language and so could not "translate" in any common meaning of the term. According to his own opaque explanation in the preface to the first edition, he "translated by the gift and power of God" (Book of Mormon [1830], v). With the plates had come a strange instrument named "interpreters" or "Urim and Thummim," words used in the Old Testament for stones put in the breastplate worn by Aaron (Exodus 28:30). Smith looked into these stones and dictated the text, first to his wife and then to other assistants.

Translation with the interpreters bears some resemblance to the folk magic practices of Smith's time. Like many other poor Yankees, Joseph Sr. was attracted to treasure-seeking, a form of magical supernaturalism then popular throughout the northeastern United States. Treasure-seekers used magical formulas and rituals but still thought of themselves as Christians. In 1822, Joseph Jr. discovered a stone that his followers said enabled him to locate lost property. Wanting to put the gift to good use, Joseph Sr. pressed his son into treasure-seeking. For four years they looked for the elusive treasures, until in 1826 Joseph Jr. was put on trial for "glass-looking," peering into the stone in search of lost objects, an illegal activity in New York because it was often practiced by swindlers. As the trial record makes clear, the Smiths were extricating themselves from treasure-seeking by then. According to a trial report, Joseph Sr. testified that he was "mortified that this wonderful power which God had so miraculously given him [Joseph Jr.] should be used only in search of filthy lucre" and prayed that God would reveal a higher use for his son's gifts.[3] By 1829, Joseph Jr. was using his seerstone, rather than the Urim and Thummim, to translate the Book of Mormon.

After a number of false starts, he began translating in earnest in April 1829 and dictated most of the 584 pages of the text in about three months. How Smith wrote the book is a subject of intense controversy. The commonsense explanation is that he composed it from scraps of information flowing in from the immediate environment and whatever reading he might have done. The finished work, however, seems far beyond the capacities of a person with little education and no writing experience, leading Mormons to believe it had to be inspired. Smith's wife Emma described what she saw as she helped with the translation.

> In writing for J[oseph]. S[mith]. I frequently wrote day after day, often sitting at the table close by him, he sitting with his face buried in his hat, with the stone in it and dictating hour after hour, with nothing between us. He had neither mss [manuscript] nor book to read from. If he had had anything of the Kind he could not have concealed it from me. The plates often lay on the table without any attempt at concealment, wrapped in a small linen table cloth, which I had given him to fold them in.[4]

The text was completed and copyrighted in June 1829.

Although critics and believers alike have found evidence of nineteenth-century religion and politics in the Book of Mormon, in its entirety it was unlike anything in his environment, save for the Bible. In fact, it is best understood as an elaboration of the Bible, extending the history of Israel to the western hemisphere. The book tells the story of a family of Israelites who left Jerusalem in 600 BCE on the eve of the Babylonian captivity. Led by the promise of a new land, they migrated to a site now thought to be on the southern coast of the Arabian peninsula, where they built a ship. Sailing eastward, they would have navigated the Indian and Pacific oceans and landed somewhere in the Americas. Here their prophets taught them the Christian gospel, while they still were practicing the Mosaic law.

The Book of Mormon is comprised of fifteen books named after prophets, much like the Bible's prophetic books named for Isaiah and Ezekiel. The book of Third Nephi contains the teachings of Christ, who visited these people in America after his resurrection. Christ established a messianic kingdom of peace and righteousness, but after two centuries this kingdom deteriorated and wars erupted. The prophets were killed, and Mormon, the general and prophet who compiled the book and gave it its name, perished in a final conflagration. Before he died, Mormon passed the golden plates containing the history to his son Moroni, who buried them sometime before his death around 421 CE. Fourteen centuries later, in 1823, Moroni appeared as an angel and told Joseph to recover the plates.

The Book of Mormon was Joseph Smith's calling card to the world. Its Christian message established him as a religious voice, not a treasure-seeker, and its seemingly miraculous production was evidence of his divine powers. No one who knew him believed he could have written the book himself. His wife expressed her wonder at this feat:

When acting as his scribe he would dictate to me hour after hour, and when returning after meals or after interruptions, he could at once begin where he had left off, without either seeing the mss or having any portion of it read to him. This was a usual thing for him to do. It would have been improbable that a learned man could do this, and for so ignorant and unlearned as he was it was simply impossible.[5]

The message of the book impressed seekers, but its existence alone awed them.

People in Manchester and nearby Palmyra tried to stop the book's publication, but a local printer finished the work in March 1830. Meanwhile stories of the plates and Joseph's revelations persuaded a few friends. On April 6, 1830, Smith organized the Church of Christ. A revelation given near the time of the organization called Smith "a seer, a translator, a prophet, an apostle of Jesus Christ, an elder of the Church through the will of God, the Father, and the grace of your Lord Jesus Christ" (Doctrine and Covenants 21:1).

The Doctrine and Covenants

Looking back over the decade from around 1820, when the First Vision occurred, to the organization of the church in 1830, the year 1828 stands out as a turning point in Joseph Smith's life. Until then he was an obscure boy with strange stories of revelations and a gift for seeing in a stone. By his own account, marvelous events had happened to him, but he had accomplished nothing. He had told almost no one about his vision of God and Christ and only his family about the angel Moroni. Nothing went down on paper.

In 1828, at age twenty-two, he began to write. He started the dictation of his apocryphal bible concerning Israelites in the western hemisphere and also began recording his other revelations, evidence of a growing self-awareness about his role as a prophet. The first written revelation was a rebuke from God for having carelessly allowed his scribe to lose 116 manuscript pages of his Book of Mormon dictation. The revelation chastised him for fearing man more than God and warned him that he could fail in his work. Other revelations came in rapid fire thereafter, telling him and his friends that a great and marvelous work was about to come forth. He kept careful written copies of them all.

Soon after he organized the church, Smith began preparing the revelations for publication. They were published as the Book of Commandments in 1833 and then revised and expanded two years later as the Doctrine and Covenants. After being presented to the church for acceptance as scripture, the Doctrine and Covenants and the Book of Mormon joined the Bible as components of the canon—and that was not the end. The Book of Mormon spoke of other branches of Israel besides those in Palestine and America receiving revelation. The book foreshadowed a time when new bibles would be forthcoming as ever more ancient records came to light. In time Smith would dictate two other ancient records, the Book of Moses, expanding on Genesis in the Bible, and the Book of Abraham, about the early life of the ancient patriarch. Besides adding another book of scripture to the Bible, the Book of Mormon established the principle of godly people everywhere receiving revelations and recording scripture. Rather than holding a monopoly on God's word, the Bible became the mother of a brood of bibles.

Smith put immense stock in the revelations. When the first batch was approved for publication, he proposed to a gathering of members that the writings were more valuable than all the riches of the earth. In his mind, they were the foundation of his authority and the source of church policy. Strangely, however, he did not treat them as if they were written by the finger of the Lord. When it came time to publish, he freely edited the words written under inspiration. Sometimes he would paste together revelations given at different times into a single text. Occasionally he inserted verses to elaborate on the meaning of the revelation. He even altered wording to reflect changes in his thinking. While the words were highly valued, they were never sacrosanct or considered (like the Qur'an) a literal transcription of God's speech.

In one of Smith's revelations, described as a preface to the first Book of Commandments, the Lord says:

> Behold, I am God and have spoken it; these commandments are of me, and were given unto my servants in their weakness, after the manner of their language, that they might come to understanding (Doctrine and Covenants 1:24).

The mind of the revelator, as well as the mind of God, participated in the revelations. Words from heaven were filtered through the language and culture of the hearers, making room for flexibility in interpretation and an occasional need to correct textual mistakes.

Smith's scriptures are less rigid than the Bible of Christian fundamentalists. Although Mormons read their scriptures as if they are listening to God, they do not think scriptures are written in the language of God, especially when the manuscripts are passed down through history. Within months after the church's organization, Smith began revising the Bible on the assumption that mistakes had crept in. He added long passages to Genesis and reworked phrases elsewhere to make more sense. In a culture that revered the Bible as God's word, it was a heaven-daring act. Smith did not publish the revised Bible in his lifetime, but it stands as a monument to his confidence in his prophetic powers.

Although Smith's authority rested on his revelations, he did not reserve revelatory gifts exclusively for himself. Revelations for the entire church must come through the head of the church, he insisted, but every person could speak a kind of scripture through the inspiration of the Holy Ghost. That certainly applied to his successors in the presidency of the church, who are believed to speak for God to the church. Church presidents from Brigham Young to the present have been regarded as prophets with the same revelatory authority as Joseph Smith. None produced revelations or new doctrine as prolifically as Smith, but Mormons believe the teachings in their discourses and writings bear divine approval. More important, Smith's visions set the pattern for everyone, including ordinary members. The visions showed God's willingness to speak to his children at all levels in the church if only they will seek him.

Revelation in Mormon life

No single doctrine distinguishes Mormonism more sharply than the belief in direct revelation. It underlies everything from the governing authority of the church to every Mormon's daily life. Smith's First Vision laid down a pattern that Mormons follow to this day. There will be confusion and doubt, his story implied, but humble prayers like his can bring light from heaven. Because of Joseph Smith's success in hearing from the Lord, every Mormon looks for guidance from above. Even Mormon children are taught to pray and to "listen to the Spirit" for answers. In their church duties, which in an organization without any professional clergy can be complicated and burdensome, Mormons are perpetually counseled to listen to the Holy Spirit.

The hope of revelation goes beyond church work. Mormons seek divine inspiration in their personal affairs, in dealing with wayward children, in managing their businesses and jobs. Mormon students pray for inspiration in their exams. Young people ask for help in choosing the right person to marry. Everyone knows that inspiration does not always come on demand, but Mormons continue to ask. If Joseph Smith was a charismatic leader who governed by virtue of his divine gifts, he also democratized that charisma. Everyone, adults and children, men and women, rich and poor, high leaders and humble followers, seeks inspiration.

Revelation provides individual Mormons with a "testimony," one of the most potent words in the Mormon lexicon. Revelation, they believe, can confirm the truth of the gospel of Christ and the words of the prophets. All the basic beliefs, including the existence of God, his willingness to answer prayers, the atonement of Christ, the prophetic calling of Joseph Smith, the veracity of the scriptures, and the continuance of revelation down to the present, are components of a standard Mormon testimony. The truth of it all can be known, they believe, by inspiration sought through prayer. Mormon missionaries want more than anything else for their prospective converts to pray for a testimony of the missionaries' teachings.

Mormons cannot explain exactly how this revelation is received. One of Joseph Smith's earliest revelations suggested that after studying it in one's mind and praying, God would "cause your bosom to burn" if it was right (Doctrine and Covenants 9:8). Another scripture less dramatically indicated that God would "speak peace to your mind" to affirm a truth (Doctrine and Covenants 6:23). The Book of Mormon suggested a gradual process of lived experience that was like planting a seed. After trying "an experiment" of opening oneself to the possibility of faith, faith, like a seed, would begin to grow and enlarge the soul. Eventually the plant would bear good fruit, evidence the original seed was good (Alma 32:27–28, 34). Most Mormons find spiritual experience, as Elijah did, in "a still small voice" rather than

Revelation at Oxford

While a Rhodes scholar at Oxford University in 1975, Clayton Christensen, now a professor at the Harvard Business School, reached a crisis in his faith where he felt he had to know if the Book of Mormon was true. Later he described the process he went through to test the book.

I reserved the time from 11:00 until midnight, every night, to read the Book of Mormon next to the fireplace in my chilly room at the Queen's College. I began each of those sessions by kneeling in verbal prayer. I told God, every single night, that I was reading the book to know if it was His truth. I told Him that I *needed* an answer to this question because if it was not true I did not want to waste my time with this church and would search for something else. But if it *was* true, then I promised that I would devote my life to following its teachings, and to helping others do the same.

I then would sit in the chair and read a page in the Book of Mormon. I would stop at the bottom of the page and think about it. I would ask myself what the material on that page meant for the way I needed to conduct my life. I would then get on my knees and pray aloud again, asking the Lord to tell me if the book was true. I would then get back in the chair, turn the page, and repeat the process for the remainder of the hour. I did this every evening.

After I had done this for several weeks, one evening in October 1975, as I sat in the chair and opened the book following my prayer, I felt a marvelous spirit come into the room and envelop my body. I had never before felt such an intense feeling of peace and love. I started to cry and did not want to stop. I knew then, from a source of understanding more powerful than anything I had ever felt in my life, that the book I was holding in my hands was true. It was hard to see through the tears. But as I opened it and began again to read, I saw in the words of the book a clarity and magnitude of God's plan for us that I had never conceived before. The spirit stayed with me for that entire hour. And each night thereafter, as I prayed and then sat in that chair with the Book of Mormon, that same spirit returned. It changed my heart and my life forever.

"Clayton Christensen," in *Why I Believe* (Salt Lake City: Bookcraft, 2002), 93–94.

dramatic manifestations (1 Kings 19:12). In the end, Mormons do not offer precise answers to the queries about revelation. They explain their own spiritual experiences and their faith as something that anyone can experience.

Testimony bears most critically on children growing up in the church. Mormons know full well that Joseph Smith's story is hard to accept. Will their children subscribe to the story of the gold plates and all that followed? Will they believe in Joseph Smith's divine calling, the truth of the revelations, the organization of an authorized church, and the descent of the prophetic office to Joseph Smith's successors? Parents know that belief imposes strict behavioral rules on their children—no smoking or drinking, no premarital sex, a two-year mission for the boys. Young Mormons have to discipline themselves to stay in the faith. And staying in the faith means a lifetime of service. With no professional clergy, the church cannot continue without the devotion of its members. Parents believe their children's willingness to sacrifice depends on getting a testimony. Will it happen?

The church program is designed to instill that testimony in the rising generation. The church sponsors Scouting, camping, youth conferences, dances, and service projects, along with weekly and sometimes daily instructional classes, all designed to keep young people within the orbit of the church and open to the influence of the Holy Spirit. Parents fear that a departure from the rules of chastity will harden the hearts of their boys and girls against the Spirit of the Lord. The sin itself can be forgiven and repairs made, but will a young person with a bad conscience stay with the church? Will knowing that they have gotten drunk or had sexual relations alienate them from church culture? Mormons fear that if sin prevents young people from getting a testimony, they will slip away. They will not marry a Mormon, at least not in the preferred way in the temple; they will not attend meetings or volunteer to serve in the church; they will not rear their own children as Mormons. Generations may be affected by decisions made at age sixteen.

Mormon parents hope and pray their children will gain testimonies that the "gospel is true." If they do, all else will fall into place. Growing children may ask questions and have doubts about particulars, just as Joseph Smith did, but if they pray and receive their own revelations, all will be well.

Mormon reason

Belief in personal inspiration seems to be a tenuous foundation on which to raise so large and complex a structure as the Church of Jesus Christ of Latter-day Saints. Would it not stand more securely on a rational basis for belief? Mormons do celebrate a kind of rationality, but always in subordination to inspiration. Mormon intellectuals have rarely engaged the philosophical theology of traditional Christian thinkers. Arguments for the existence of God figure very little in Mormon thinking. Mormons are more likely to believe that philosophical influence corrupted Christianity rather than providing a sound basis for belief. Until recently, few Mormon thinkers have investigated the philosophical foundations of Mormonism.

Mormons are more attracted to the empirical traditions of science. They have made elaborate attempts to prove the Book of Mormon, just as nineteenth-century Christian apologists marshaled evidence in support of the Bible. The presentation of evidence began with Joseph Smith himself before the organization of the church in 1830. Smith had been instructed to conceal the gold plates from curious onlookers, presumably as a safety measure. Initially no one saw them directly, not even his wife, though she felt them wrapped in a linen cloth on the table. Since, according to Smith's account, the plates were returned to the angel and are no longer accessible, their very existence is in doubt. One critical historian has postulated that Smith manufactured bogus plates out of tin and moved them about wrapped in a cloth to deceive his followers. To answer the critics, Joseph Smith showed the plates to two groups of men, three in the first group and eight in the second. Besides seeing the plates, the group of eight handled them, and all

31

subscribed to a testimony published in every copy of the Book of Mormon as a sort of legal proof that the plates existed.

From that day on, Mormons have collected evidence in support of the Joseph Smith story and more particularly the Book of Mormon. In the complex of Mormon belief, no other item is so susceptible to historical analysis. A vision of God to Joseph Smith is no more testable than a vision to Paul or Elijah. But a history of a migrant band of Israelites to America is open to investigation. Is there archaeological evidence of their civilization? Do their practices conform to what is known of ancient Near Eastern and American life? Could the Book of Mormon have emerged from antiquity, or does it bear signs of nineteenth-century origins?

These questions have generated a huge literature. Critics claim that there is no archaeological evidence for Book of Mormon civilizations and that everything in the book can be traced to Joseph Smith's nineteenth-century environment. Mormon scholars assert the opposite. They have produced vast amounts of evidence for the Book of Mormon's historical authenticity. They have, for example, located a site on the route of Book of Mormon people on the Arabian peninsula bearing the same name as one assigned in the Book of Mormon—a name unknown in Joseph Smith's time. The opening pages of the Book of Mormon relate a vision of God sitting on his throne that follows closely the pattern of throne visions found in ancient literatures. Certain passages in the Book of Mormon follow the scriptural form of chiasmus, a technical term referring to a sequence of statements reaching a climax at a midpoint and then repeating the same sequence in reverse order to the end. The Bible is laced with chiasmic writing, and so is the Book of Mormon. Although such pieces of evidence are small taken individually, cumulatively they impress Mormon rationalists.

Mormons say these resemblances to antiquity are too remarkable to be coincidences. Mormon philanthropy in league with these

Mormon scholars has created one institution after another to pursue proof of the Book of Mormon. In recent years, the Foundation for Ancient Research and Modern Studies (FARMS), now part of Brigham Young University, has produced hundreds of publications in defense of the book. Many Mormons are persuaded that the evidence is overwhelming.

The debate resembles the battles over archaeological evidence for the Bible. Evangelical Christians claim the proof is convincing, while critical archaeologists are skeptical. Facts are assembled, arguments mounted, and neither side persuades the other. The Mormon apologists, however, differ from their counterparts in other Christian groups. Mormons collect the evidence and make the arguments but believe that in the last analysis faith is gained through life experiences, not through research and argumentation. Perfect proof for religious beliefs, the Mormon rationalists say, can never be assembled. They don't believe because of their researches, they say, but because of the Spirit.

One commentator after another has predicted that Mormonism will crumble because of its foundation in personal inspiration. How can Mormons survive educated doubt and scientific inquiry? Many Mormons do falter in the face of opposing arguments, but defection from the church does not correlate with level of education. Survey data show that Latter-day Saints with PhD's are more likely to be fully practicing than high school graduates. The combination of evidence and Mormonism's culture of inspiration holds the allegiance of all kinds of people.

This broad spectrum of believers may result partly from the trust that Mormons put in their own thinking. At bottom, Mormons think that each person must choose what to believe. In favoring inspiration over reason, Mormons transfer responsibility for finding the truth away from the most knowing—the scientists and scholars—and onto themselves. One cannot rely on experts in theology or science to discover principles to live by. For the most

33

fundamental matters of personal belief, each person must consult his or her own inspiration. Just as Joseph Smith learned of the truth about the churches by going directly to God, individual Mormons must rely on their own capacity for inspiration. Mormon parents worry about their children developing faith but know that in the end the outcome is between them and God.

Chapter 3
Zion

The Mormon people

It has been said that Joseph Smith's greatest creation was the Mormon people. Even observers who have little use for Smith's doctrines applaud the Latter-day Saints' unity and communality. The *Harvard Encyclopedia of American Ethnic Groups* (1980) includes a long entry on the Mormons, one of the few groups in the volume whose inclusion is based on religion rather than national origins or common ancestry. Surveying the entire range of social configurations that evolved within America, the sociologist Thomas F. O'Dea observed that the Mormons "came closer to evolving an ethnic identity on this continent than any other group."[1]

Mormons like to think of themselves as a peculiar people with an overarching identity. If asked who they are, many church members rank their Mormonism above race, national origin, class, or vocation. In support of their religious identity, Mormons contribute 10 percent of their annual income to the church, may work ten or fifteen hours a week in unpaid church service, and go on voluntary two-year missions without pay. They feel immense loyalty to one another and to the organization they serve.

Mormonism's peculiar beliefs in themselves draw Mormons together. Smith's revelations raise such a high barrier to belief that anyone who accepts them inevitably becomes an insider. In accepting Smith's revelations, believers embrace all that follows: the authority of the church, the succession of prophetic leadership down to the current president, and the obligation to live Mormon teachings. Common belief establishes trust and a sense of mutual responsibility. Mormons pride themselves on feeling at home with other church members anywhere in the world. Lost in a foreign land, Mormons would expect assistance from any Mormon they happened to meet.

Zion

Communality is more than a by-product of Mormon doctrines. From the beginning, Mormons have actively sought unity. They aspire to be a people, thinking of themselves as a society as much as a church. Their common ground goes beyond belief and worship to work, education, family, and business. This comprehensiveness goes back to their origins, when Joseph Smith first organized the church.

It was evident within a year after the church's organization in April 1830 that Smith wanted to create a society that was more than congregations of worshippers. Protestantism spread westward in this period by organizing people for Sunday worship with a clergyman to preach and administer the sacraments. Outside of these church meetings, Protestants blended with the rest of the American populace. Smith went beyond congregational worship to the organization of cities and the formation of complete societies.

In the fall of 1830, he began to receive revelations about the construction of a "New Jerusalem," referring to the holy city in the Revelation of St. John that was to descend from heaven in the last day (Revelation 21:10). The city, which the Mormons also called the City of Zion or just Zion, was to be a godly society worthy of Christ at his coming. In July 1831, a revelation designated Independence, Missouri, at the outer edge of white settlement, as the place for the city, and Mormons began to buy land in surrounding Jackson County where church members could gather.

The motives for founding Zion sprang from the Mormon sense of time. Like many Protestants in that period, Mormons thought they lived on the eve of the Second Coming. William Miller, the

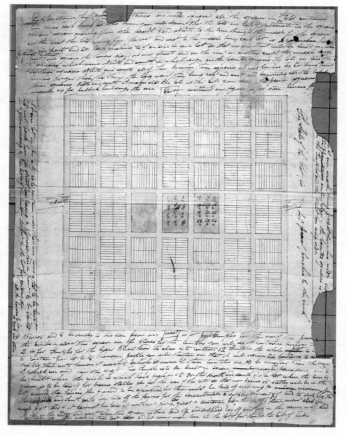

3. Plat of the City of Zion prepared by Joseph Smith and his counselor Frederick G. Williams in 1832.

self-taught New York student of the Bible who predicted that Christ would return in 1843, began preaching his calendar of the Second Coming in 1831. The millenarians foresaw all sorts of calamities: wars, pestilence, natural disasters, and human cruelty. They believed that the old order was on the verge of collapse and a new order was emerging. For Mormons, the City of Zion was to be a place of refuge in a turbulent world. They were to gather into the city for their own safety as well as to build a righteous society. The little congregations that sprang up in the wake of Mormon missionary efforts were only to be temporary stopping places until the converts could gather to Zion.

A Mormon scripture describing the ancient city of Enoch became a model for the modern Saints. Enoch's city was a Zion "because they were of one heart and one mind, and dwelt in righteousness; and there was no poor among them" (Book of Moses 7:18). Even before Independence was designated as the site for the city, a revelation instructed members of the church to pool their property in order to eliminate poverty. On coming to Zion, each person was to deed all he owned to the bishop, who would deed back an amount suitable to the circumstances of the person, thereby equalizing wealth among the membership. No one was to suffer for lack of land or of tools to practice a trade. To maintain equality, each year families were to return their surplus "income," whether cash or produce, to the bishop. These properties were to be used for public works and to supply a livelihood to new arrivals. With the reforms went an ethic of simple living: the Saints were to live a plain life. "Thou shalt not be proud in thy heart; let all thy garments be plain, and their beauty the beauty of the work of thine own hands" (Doctrine and Covenants 42:42).

In places, Smith's scriptures condemned inequality as a dire evil. "It is not given that one man should possess that which is above another, wherefore the world lieth in sin" (Doctrine and Covenants 49:20). "If ye are not equal in earthly things ye cannot be equal in obtaining heavenly things" (Doctrine and Covenants 78:6).

But the impracticality of the equalization principle eventually forced a compromise. Even with the best will in the world, the early converts lacked the means to make the system work. There were too few rich and too many poor. Equalization would have impoverished everyone, and the small number of propertied people hung back. Smith berated the unwilling rich in his eagerness to conform to the revelation, but eventually he compromised.

The consecration of properties as prescribed in the revelation for Zion was practiced in Independence for two years, but in subsequent gathering places, Smith installed it only in attenuated form as an annual tithe of income or as cooperative production projects. In Nauvoo, where he had more resources and more influence than ever before, he made no effort to implement economic communitarianism. Brigham Young instituted a consecration program in Utah, but it foundered due to a lack of organized capital and the disruptions caused by political struggles with the federal government.

Consecration today

Over time, the consecration of properties was transmuted into a more general attitude that underlies Mormon charitable works to the present day. The consecration principle instills an obligation to devote one's means to help the poor and build the church. Like other Christian groups, Mormons consider property a stewardship entrusted to individuals to advance God's purposes. In practical terms, after full consecration ended, the revelations commanded Mormons to tithe their annual income. Fully engaged Mormons today (probably a quarter to a third of the membership) contribute 10 percent of their income to the church. Tithe-paying is a requirement for entrance into Mormon temples, the special buildings only dedicated Mormons are allowed to enter. Each year the bishop, the lay leader of each congregation, interviews individual Mormons to determine if they have paid a full tithe.

No exact definition of a tithe is specified. Is income tithed before or after taxes? Are business expenses excluded from tithing? What about contributions to other charities? The bishop makes no inquiries into the method of calculating a tithe, and the church offers no official definition. Each tithe-payer determines for himself or herself if the tithe is full or not. But loosely defined though it be, tithing is a basic component of faithful Mormon practice.

Out of the early Zion principles also evolved the Mormon sense of how to care for the poor. The scriptural condemnation of inequality in the early years was less an attack on the systemic inequalities of capitalism than an admonition to watch over the needy. In the twentieth century, the consecration principle took the form of a welfare program begun during the Great Depression to provide work and sustenance for poor church members. The church now owns farms, canning plants, and manufacturing facilities where the poor work producing the goods they need to subsist. By managing the production of goods, the church can offer jobs to the poor as well as food and clothing, the aim being to make them self-sufficient. To supplement this system of production, cash offerings are collected to pay for rent and gasoline.

Anyone in need can approach the bishop of his or her congregation and receive an order for goods from a church storehouse. In outlying areas where the Mormon population is widely scattered, members pick up food from regional storehouses and bring it to church meetinghouses for distribution. The bishop tries to incorporate food and clothing into a larger program of rehabilitation, which usually includes service in the church.

Outside of the welfare system, the modern church manages a variety of humanitarian aid programs around the world. Aid is extended regardless of the recipients' religion and is frequently distributed in cooperation with the charitable relief arms of other faiths. Among hundreds of efforts, the church shipped supplies to

4. In 2005, the Church sent food packages from the supplies in its storehouses to victims of Hurricane Katrina.

the tsunami victims around the Indian Ocean in 2004 and to families hurt by mudslides in Honduras in 1998. In addition to the official programs, thousands of Mormons are involved in private philanthropic organizations for sending doctors to deprived areas, helping to build water systems in African villages, and teaching English in emerging nations. Mormons have been especially attracted to the microcredit movement, granting small loans to hardworking poor people to develop their own small businesses. This combination of charity and self-help appeals to Mormons because it reflects the church's preference for teaching self-sufficiency over outright handouts. Brigham Young University has become a major academic center for the microcredit movement.

In 2001, the church drew on its experience with microcredit to launch the Perpetual Education Fund (PEF). Invoking the memory of the nineteenth-century Perpetual Emigrating Fund, which advanced loans to help European Mormons migrate to the western United States, the modern PEF extends educational loans to thousands of young Mormons in Latin America, Africa, and the South Pacific, many of them former missionaries. Initially funded from voluntary donations by North American Mormons, the fund aims to become self-perpetuating as its beneficiaries repay their loans.

In the long view, Mormons think of tithing and the welfare program as interim measures. Mormons still believe they may return to the city of Zion in Missouri as the Second Coming approaches. At that time, a full consecration of properties will be required again, and everyone will be put on an equal footing. No one knows when this mythic return may occur, but it represents the sense that a higher law hovers over temporal dealings even now. Someday the Lord will require everything of his people as he once did in Missouri.

Opposition

The City of Zion as originally envisioned was never built. Zion has functioned more as an ideal in Mormon history than as a realized actuality. Wherever the Mormons settled, local animosity forced them to leave. By the time they left Illinois for the West in 1846, they had been evicted from four of their primary settlements. By the end of Joseph Smith's lifetime, Mormons thought of themselves as a persecuted people. Memories of hardship, suffering, and the opposition of a hostile world became a large part of Mormon identity.

The Mormons had been gathering in Missouri for less than two years when growing animosity broke out in violence. Because the Mormons had not broken any laws, Jackson County resorted to vigilantism. To remove them, local citizens demanded that the Mormons depart within six months, tarred and feathered the bishop, and destroyed the Mormon printing press. Under duress the Mormons signed an agreement to leave, and then consulted a lawyer in hopes of obtaining legal redress. Enraged at this act of resistance, the citizens attacked Mormon cabins, pried off the roofs to expose families to the November cold, and whipped the men. By the end of 1833, the Mormons had fled the county. The citizens refused to let them back even to negotiate the sale of their property.

The Missourians complained that an article in the Mormon newspaper in Jackson County had encouraged the importation of free blacks, which was anathema in slaveholding Missouri. Mormons claimed they were only warning future immigrants of the legal obstacles free blacks would face. The citizens had a number of other objections, but their main fear was the rising Mormon population, which threatened to swamp the non-Mormon citizens and put Mormons in control of public offices. In 1833, fearful citizens in Independence issued a manifesto explaining why they had to take drastic action: "What would be the fate of our lives and property, in the hands of jurors & witnesses, who do not blush to declare and would not upon occasion hesitate to swear, that they have wrought miracles, and have been the subjects of miracles and supernatural cures; have converse with God and his Angels, and possess and exercise gifts of Divination and of unknown tongues."[2] The Missourians feared their lives would soon be at the mercy of religious fanatics.

Wherever Mormons settled they met specific accusations—collusion with Indians, interference with slaves, theft, counterfeiting—but underlying them all was this fear of fanatics in power. Joseph Smith's enemies linked him to Muhammad, the arch-fanatic in the nineteenth-century imagination. Both men claimed to speak for God through revelation, and the logic of the prevailing stereotype implied they would impose their views on everyone else. It was to demonstrate their religion's tolerance that the Nauvoo City Council, at Joseph Smith's prompting, passed the ordinance to admit people of every religion, including Catholics, Jews, and "Muhammadans." He included the right of all men to worship God according to the dictates of their own consciences in the thirteen basic articles of faith, but his enemies were convinced that he aimed to make himself a religious dictator, an American pope.

The Mormons felt helpless in the face of their enemies. They appealed to local courts, to the governor, and repeatedly to the president of the United States, all without success. Officials usually told the Saints to enter complaints against their attackers in the courts, but enmity was so high that they could not hope for a fair trial; often their opponents prevented witnesses from testifying. Only rarely was a judgment handed down in their favor or did a state militia officer or justice of the peace come to their defense. Much of the time Mormons existed in a state of undeclared war with their neighbors, in which all normal legal procedures were suspended.

Occasionally the Mormons were advised to defend themselves by force, and in 1838 they took this counsel to heart. One of Smith's close associates, his counselor Sidney Rigdon, warned would-be attackers that they would meet resistance and destruction at Mormon hands. Mormons backed up their threats with the organization of a county militia under Mormon control and the formation of a band of vigilantes called Danites, after one of the more militant tribes of Israel, to take action against their enemies. After repeated harassments and threats, the Mormons drove suspected attackers out of the areas where Mormons had settled, adopting the very tactics used by their enemies: vigilante action. The results were disastrous. The governor issued a proclamation expelling the Mormons from the state. The body of Saints fled Missouri for Illinois, and Joseph Smith was thrown in jail on charges of treason for resisting the state militia.

The repeated defeats poisoned Mormon memory, but they also bound the Mormons to one another. The Mormons began to think of themselves as a persecuted minority as well as the bearers of glad tidings of the restoration. Smith told visitors the pitiful story of their ill treatment as often as he narrated his revelations. The Mormons were like Christians of old, persecuted for Christ's sake. For all the bitterness they caused, the wrongs united the Mormons, making them depend on each other because they could depend on no one else.

Building Zion

The Mormons could have placated their enemies by not collecting in such large numbers. The Independence citizenry would have tolerated a handful of Mormons gathering to worship in a small church. It was the influx of hundreds of Mormons and the prospect of even more coming that precipitated the attacks. Friendly non-Mormons advised Joseph Smith that dispersing his followers would calm the opposition. But an end to gathering was out of the question. The revelations charged the church to gather Israel from across the earth as part of the divine plan to recover God's lost people. The City of Zion was to be a New Jerusalem, a Jerusalem for the New World. Zion was both the place of refuge from calamity and the place of divine instruction where a latter-day temple was to be built. To stop gathering would defeat one of early Mormonism's fundamental purposes.

Even as persecution forced Mormons in upon themselves, they united in an expansive outward movement to carry the gospel to the world and gather people to Zion. Joseph Smith dispatched missionaries the moment the church was organized in 1830, and the proselytizing has never stopped. In 1837, in the midst of some of his greatest difficulties, he sent a number of his most loyal associates to Great Britain. Eventually a majority of the Mormons who settled in the western United States would be Britons, Scandinavians, and other Europeans.

Because of scanty records, the exact nature of the early missionaries' message is hard to recover. Receiving little instruction from Smith, they must have drawn on their background in other churches for teaching the standard Christian gospel. It is known that they emphasized spiritual gifts and revelation to a modern prophet. They proclaimed that God had restored the authority and power of the New Testament Christian church; prophets and apostles were reenacting the Book of Acts. They also brought news of Israel gathering to Zion in fulfillment of Old Testament prophecy: The city was being constructed now in the West as a place of refuge against the storms and trials of the premillennial period.

Though never repudiated or entirely forgotten, the millennial message lost its urgency as the years went by. The signal message became the restoration of the primitive gospel to power and authority after centuries of apostasy. The missionaries emphasized the principles taught on the day of Pentecost in the Book of Acts: faith, repentance, baptism by immersion, and the gift of the Holy Ghost by the laying on of hands. This simple message, coming straight out of the New Testament, appealed to people steeped in the Bible.

The missionary impulse has never receded in Mormon culture. Today's Mormon boys feel an obligation to enter the mission field at age nineteen. For two years they walk the streets looking for people willing to listen. In some areas, one or two baptisms a year per missionary is the norm, and the numbers are rarely very high. The missionaries themselves, or more often their families, pay the costs, usually around five hundred dollars a month. There are no stipends. The missionaries and their families consider this service an obligation and privilege flowing from the consecration of their lives to God.

In the twentieth century, a growing number of young women began to join the missionary ranks, though their obligation is less keenly felt. For the young men, going on a mission is both a rite of passage and a test of developing faithfulness. Although there are social pressures, every young Latter-day Saint man has to decide for himself about a mission. For those who go, the mission cements their Latter-day Saint identity. They have time to investigate the scriptures and Mormon doctrine and learn what it means to serve selflessly under difficult circumstances. The hardships of missionary work function as a form of initiation. Although some defect from the church after their return, the large majority enter

5. Clad in trademark white shirts, a pair of young missionaries visits a family in the South Pacific.

into the round of church service that fills Latter-day Saint lives. The missions are the training ground for the next generation of Mormon leaders.

Modern missionaries teach a simple gospel of faith in Christ and the restoration of the church. They tell their prospects (called investigators) the story of Joseph Smith and assure them that if they will pray humbly, they will receive a spiritual confirmation. Then the investigators are urged to repent of their sins, which among other things means they will have no sex outside marriage and will refrain from tea, coffee, tobacco, and alcohol. Adherence to these rather difficult and in some cases foreign standards of conduct measures the sincerity of conversion. The basic question is whether the investigator believes enough to change his or her life.

Converts no longer gather to Mormon strongholds as they once almost invariably did. The requirement of moving to Zion was suspended at the end of the nineteenth century. So long as Utah and the surrounding states needed new settlers, gathering made sense. It enabled Mormons to create a culture of their own in the recesses of the Great Basin. But as the Utah economy reached its limits, the impulse to gather weakened. Church leaders instructed new converts to stay in their home areas and build up the church.

By the end of the twentieth century, converts understood that their first obligation was to advance the work in their native areas. Joseph Smith had always spoken of Zion as an expansive idea. Once one city was constructed, his instructions to the people in Jackson County had explained, other such cities were to be built until the world was filled with Zion. Smith dreamed of an array of cities, initially in the United States and then in all of the Americas, extending Zion to the rest of the world. Converts now gather to multiple Zions planted in every land.

Although the meaning of Zion has changed over the century and three-quarters since the Mormons founded their first city in Missouri, out of that initial Zion came many of Mormonism's fundamental features: consecration of property, a story of persecutions, and the charge to gather Israel. None of these exists now in its original form. Consecration has become a general principle of willingness to serve in the church, care for the poor, and tithe income. The experience of persecution has turned into a memory of heroic struggle. Missionaries no longer gather people to Zion or offer refuge against the calamities of the last day; they invite people into the multiple Zions in local congregations throughout the world.

But even in their transformed state, those impulses still tie Mormons to one another. The society Joseph Smith set out to create survived intense opposition in the nineteenth century and adapted to rapid change and global expansion in the twentieth. Mormons still think of their congregations as places of peace, equality, and unity, and of themselves as a distinctive people. They still believe that some day a full-blown Zion will arise in which the people of God will constitute a righteous society.

Chapter 4
Priesthood

Restoration of authority

Joseph Smith revived a question that had troubled Protestant reformers for centuries: Whence the authority to act for God? The Roman Catholics had a simple answer: Their priesthood descended from Peter. Every bishop of Rome since Peter traced his authority back to Christ's chief apostle. After the Reformation separated Protestants from Catholics, the reformers faced a perplexing problem: Could they trace their authority through a church they had rejected? Were Protestant priests and elders authorized to administer the sacraments without holding the priesthood handed down through the Roman church? An urgent question in the seventeenth century, the issue had receded by Joseph Smith's time. The radical Protestants around the Smith family considered success in preaching sufficient evidence of a divine call. Most churches ordained preachers without particular concern for the lineage of clerical authority.

Smith revived the question of authority by reestablishing a link to the priestly authority of the New Testament. Two of his most significant early revelations dealt with priesthood. In his 1838 history, he told of John the Baptist appearing to him and his translation scribe, Oliver Cowdery, in May 1829 to bestow the Levitical priesthood of ancient Israel. According to Smith, John came to the two men as they prayed about baptism. He laid hands on their heads and said he was conferring the priesthood of Aaron on them, authorizing them to baptize people into the church. Later, in another visitation, Cowdery and Smith received the authority to bestow the gift of the Holy Ghost as described in the New Testament. A direct account of the bestowal of this second priesthood does not exist, but an 1830 revelation referred to the apostles Peter, James, and John conferring the keys of the apostleship. This second priesthood, considered the higher of the two, was named for Melchizedek, an ancient high priest in Abraham's time (Genesis 14:18–20). Smith almost immediately began conferring priesthood authority on all the adult male members of the church.

The names Aaronic and Melchizedek suggest the models for Smith's priesthoods: not Roman Catholicism, with its array of priesthood offices, but the biblical discussions of priesthood in the Epistle to the Hebrews and in Exodus. Smith dismissed Christian history as a source of authority and returned to the Old and New Testaments. Instead of depending on the descent of priesthood through the centuries, priesthood came directly from John, who baptized Christ, and from the three lead apostles, Peter, James, and John, who received the keys from Christ. Smith honored the Catholic principle of priesthood but circumvented the Catholic Church, reaching back independently to the sources of priesthood in the Bible.

The priesthood has administrative functions in Mormonism, as it does in Catholicism, but its primary functions are sacral. Priesthood holders can administer sacraments such as baptism and the laying on of hands for the gift of the Holy Ghost. To be recognized by God, a baptism in Mormonism must be performed by a person who has authority. The same is true for blessing the sacrament of the Lord's Supper, conferring priesthood, performing marriages for eternity, and anointing the sick. The ordinances are of no effect, in the Mormon view, if not performed by a holder of the priesthood. The bestowal of priesthood by heavenly messengers thus becomes the most crucial act of the restoration. With such bestowal, divine authority, lost after the death of the original apostles, returned to the earth.

Church administration

This sacral power of priesthood intermingles with the administrative structure of the church. As in Catholicism, church officials are not just bureaucratic functionaries but priests with authority to administer holy ordinances. The office of president, the highest office in the church hierarchy, is combined with the office of president of the High or Melchizedek Priesthood. For Mormons, he holds the same authority vested in Peter by Christ in Matthew 16:18–19: "whatsoever thou shalt bind on earth shall be bound in heaven." The "keys of the kingdom," in the Mormon view, include authority to bind people in family relationships that endure into the next life as well to administer all of the gospel sacraments. The president of the church holds all of these keys. His priestly authority, added to the right to revelation for the church, invests this single individual with immense power.

Faithful Mormons have great respect for the office and the man. They listen closely to his pronouncements and willingly follow his directives. He is often referred to as "the Prophet," meaning he is the spokesman for the Lord in the governance of the church. Because so much power is vested in this one figure, church authority is highly centralized. What is most difficult to comprehend about Mormonism is how this concentration of authority at the top is compatible with its democratic opposite: the dispersal of authority to millions of individual members in every congregation. While it would seem that the Prophet has all the say in running the organization, in actuality every practicing member is deeply involved in its administration. The church is simultaneously hierarchical and democratic.

The apparent contradiction began with Joseph Smith's practice of assembling councils for determining church policy. From the earliest years, he collected people into councils to help transact business. As the church organization evolved, these informal councils were institutionalized. The church president is a member of a council of three, called the First Presidency, consisting of himself and two counselors. Just below them is a Quorum of Twelve Apostles with authority to administer the affairs of the worldwide church, and below them are Councils of Seventy (a name taken from Luke 10:1 in the New Testament) who have specific responsibilities for particular regions and departments.

The revelation on priesthood organization admonishes these councils to act unanimously in making decisions, and that affects the tone of church administration at every level. While great deference is shown to those in charge, in fact the leaders of the councils must pay heed to the views of council members. They must hear all the voices and strive for unanimity even though this may delay action for long periods. Although theoretically authorized to act autocratically, the church president has to consider the views of those around him.

Beyond the "general authorities," the councils that supervise the church as a whole, responsibility for local governance is vested entirely in the laity. There is no professional clergy to pastor the church's tens of thousands of congregations. Even the general authorities pursued secular careers before they were appointed to full-time service. Each local congregation is headed by a bishop, a male chosen from the congregation to serve for five or six years while continuing his regular employment. He receives no pay and has no paid assistants. All the offices in the congregation—called a "ward" in recognition that Zion ideally is a city—are staffed by volunteers like himself. One of the bishop's chief responsibilities is to call ward members to fill positions as his counselors, ward clerks, and the presidents and staffs of priesthood groups and auxiliary organizations for women (the Relief Society), Sunday School, youth

(Young Men and Young Women), children (the Primary), Scouting, family history research, music, and so on. Most wards are composed of four or five hundred men, women, and children and require two hundred or more people to staff the organization. Everyone is expected to take an assignment, referred to as a "calling," none with remuneration. Holding a church job as well as following church standards constitutes the definition of being "active" in the church.

The presidents of stakes, groupings of five to fifteen wards, are also laypeople who maintain regular employment while fulfilling their church responsibilities. The name "stake" comes from a passage in Isaiah that compares Zion to a tent that will enlarge as new stakes are planted. Like all other church leaders, the stake president has two counselors. A twelve-man high council ratifies all important decisions.

Besides this administrative democracy, the sacral authority of the priesthood is widely distributed. All adult men are expected to make themselves worthy of the Melchizedek Priesthood. Boys are made deacons in the Aaronic Priesthood at age twelve, teachers (a priesthood office that includes visiting individual families to teach them) at fourteen, and priests at age sixteen with authority to baptize and administer the Lord's Supper, referred to in Mormon parlance as "the Sacrament." Fathers baptize their own children and confer the gift of the Holy Ghost. One of the chief duties of ward leaders is to prepare every boy and man to receive the priesthood. The aim is to invest every male with priesthood authority. The priesthood in local congregations forms a hierarchy, but one based on age and experience rather than education or wealth. Everyone has a place in the hierarchy and can look forward to moving up and assuming new offices by living faithfully and accepting callings as the bishop issues them. The people do not exist in a mass of voters over against elected officials as in a democracy; they are all officials of a kind, occupying positions in the church's administrative structure. The members exercise power not as "the people" but as officeholders themselves.

Elections and voting play a minor role in church government. Most appointments come from the level above in the hierarchy. The church president chooses his own counselors and with their concurrence selects the Twelve Apostles. Stake presidents choose the bishops, bishops the ward leaders, and so on. The names of called officers are always presented to the people for confirmation, and every six months the president of the church and the Twelve Apostles are themselves "sustained" in general conference by the congregation, including men, women, and children, raising their hands. But there is no competition for office, no parties, no campaigning. The vote is usually unanimous. It is more a show of support than an election. If a person does raise his or her hand against a proposed appointment, the presiding authority will usually consult with the dissenter to hear complaints and reconsider the decision. The people have a voice but not the last word. God speaking through his servants is sovereign, not the people.

The outcome is an organization with an intense concentration of authority at the center coupled with the diffusion of administrative authority to every active adult. Mormons may honor their Prophet as chief revelator and holder of priesthood keys, but the members are the ones who administer the church. Most men hold the priesthood, and most women have church callings. Each individual member is strongly encouraged to seek revelation for his or her calling and life. The same inspiration that is thought to lead the church president is accessible to every member. Although governing rules and general policy come down from above, ordinary members have a strong sense of possession. They own the church at the local level. Joseph Smith's refusal to create a professional clergy and instead to disperse authority to every member may be the primary sociological reason for Mormonism's success.

Mormon women are keenly aware that that they do not hold the priesthood. They do not sit on the dais as bishops or bishops' counselors. Photographs of the general authorities show only a handful of women, the dozen or so who head the women's and children's "auxiliary" organizations, at the edges of the picture. Their voices are not routinely heard in the leading councils of the church, where power is exclusively male.

Although many would like to be heard more, women are not without influence. They run the Relief Society, the Young Women, and the Primary, the auxiliary organizations for women, teenage girls, and children. They pray and preach nearly as often as the men. They officiate in the ceremonies of the temple. On the whole, women are more active in the church than men. They claim ownership and do their part with equal or superior zeal. They seek revelation from God in the same expectation of answers as the male priesthood. Whether they will eventually receive more authority and more voice is an open question.

Temples

On the sacral side of Latter-day Saint priesthood, the culminating activities take place in the temple, the most mysterious and holy of Mormon buildings. There the priesthood administers the most exalted ordinances in the Mormon panoply of sacraments, none of them accessible to nonmembers or even to less active Mormons. Mormons are instructed not to discuss the ordinances, even among themselves, outside the temple's walls.

Temple ceremonies expanded gradually over Joseph Smith's fourteen years as church president. He never explained where his interest in temples came from initially. None of the religions in his immediate environment had temples. Freemasons later built temples, but in Smith's time they set up their lodges in taverns and assembly halls. Smith's reading of the Bible is the most likely source of his inspiration—along with the revelations that mentioned temples soon after the organization of the church. The 1831 revelation on the city of Zion in Missouri called for a temple in

Independence. After that it was assumed that each of the cities of Zion would have a temple. One of Joseph Smith's first acts as cities were founded was to locate a temple site. Likewise, Brigham Young marked a place within days after arriving in the Salt Lake Valley.

Smith built temples in preference to any other kind of building. When his followers saw the need for a small chapel in Kirtland, Ohio, to accommodate the growing Mormon population, Smith proposed an immense temple instead. He never constructed an ordinary chapel in his life. The Kirtland Temple, like the others he planned, incorporated meeting spaces within its walls but served other purposes as well. The two temples he constructed had two meeting spaces stacked on top of one another with altars at each end of the rooms. The attic above held church offices that doubled as rooms for ritual instruction.

As the time for dedication of the Kirtland Temple drew near, Smith began to perform ceremonies patterned after the ordination of priests in the book of Exodus. Every worthy male received ordinances reserved for the sons of Aaron in the Old Testament, as if his people were a nation of priests. In Kirtland, the elders were ritually washed, anointed, and sealed as part of a purification ceremony to prepare them for an "endowment of power" like the showering of the Spirit on the day of Pentecost in the Book of Acts. Not long after the dedication of the Kirtland Temple on March 27, 1836, this outpouring occurred. The Mormons washed each other's feet, prayed, prophesied, saw visions, and testified that the power of God filled the temple room where they were meeting.

Six years later, a second phase was added to the temple ceremony. In 1842, Smith was initiated into the Nauvoo lodge of Freemasons, and shortly thereafter he administered an "endowment" ceremony that resembled the rituals of Freemasonry in a few outward forms but was very much an original creation. Among other significant differences from

6. The temple in Kirtland, Ohio, completed in 1836 and still standing, in a 1907 photo by the Mormon photographer George Anderson.

Freemasonry, women were included as full participants. The ceremony dramatically reenacted the Christian story of the Fall and the progressive return to God through the redemption of Christ and the acceptance of covenants. As part of the temple ceremony, Mormons were clothed in a holy garment inspired by the one Aaron wore in Exodus as part of his sanctification. Today Mormons wear these garments under their street clothes as a reminder of their covenants.

In Nauvoo, temple ceremonies and ordinary Sunday worship took place in the same building. In Utah, that mixture ended. The more than 120 temples around the world today are dedicated solely to temple ceremonies. No Sunday services occur there. They are sacred spaces set apart from the rest of the world, with an other-worldly architecture and the very best craftsmanship. The Salt Lake Temple took forty years to build, delayed in part by Brigham Young's insistence on the most sturdy construction and the finest materials. The temples' sometimes flamboyant architectural style goes far beyond the plain style of the severely functional Mormon chapels.

Mormons have become expert in creating sacred space in the midst of unlikely circumstances. In New York City, the temple stands on Broadway across from Lincoln Center; Mormons come right off the sidewalk into the temple's precincts. The sense of holy seclusion begins with admission. Everyone is welcome to weekly meetings in the thousands of chapels around the world; only "worthy" Latter-day Saints are admitted to the temple. To gain admission, a member answers a set of questions from the ward bishop and receives a "recommend" to be shown upon admission. The interview and recommend remind temple-goers that they are entering another world.

Once inside, the patrons change from their street clothes into simple white clothing. Conversation is conducted in whispers. Most of the time there is no talking, except as the ceremony requires. At the end of the almost two-hour ceremony, the worshippers gather in the celestial room, where they may review what they have experienced. Otherwise they rarely speak of the ceremonies. Outside the temple, only oblique references are made to the words of the endowment. The ceremonies are considered too holy for speech except in the temple itself. In a church with very little ceremony in its usual Sunday services, the contrast is stark.

The temples represent the culmination of Mormon life as well as Mormon worship. They are the goal toward which parents steer their children from the day they are born. Mormon parents can sum up their highest hopes for their children by saying they want them married in the temple. That implies the children have lived the rigorous Mormon lifestyle, have chosen a worthy Mormon mate, and are willing to enter into the demanding covenants of the temple endowment. A temple marriage implies future faithfulness and a desire to resist the lure of worldliness.

Marriage in the temple perpetuates the Mormon way of life: Another family is formed that will instill the gospel in its children. The implications reverberate into eternity. One of Joseph Smith's revelations sketched a vision of families continuing forever. In the temple, husbands and wives are sealed to each other and children to their parents for eternity. The implication of the eternal marriage revelation is that other institutional forms, including the church, might disappear, but the family will endure. The family is the foundation of heavenly society with God as the Father of all. In Mormon doctrine, family is the highest way of life.

However inspiring for young couples, the doctrine sometimes troubles single adults. Mormon girls grow up with the expectation that marriage to a worthy Mormon man is the highest form of a good life. What are they to make of themselves if at age thirty-five they are still unmarried? Some Mormon girls fail to prepare for a career in the expectation of an early marriage. Even those with serious careers and many achievements wonder about their state as single women. Such uncertainties, common to single women of every belief, are magnified by the doctrine of eternal marriage.

Single men's concerns take a different form. They know it is their responsibility to take the initiative. If they fail to find wives, they are at fault. In urban areas, the church organizes wards composed solely of single young people in hopes of facilitating engagements. The number of marriages coming out of the singles wards justifies their existence, but they also ghettoize their members. Gay Mormons feel even more isolated. The church insists they remain both chaste and celibate. Finding their position untenable, many drop out of church activity. Some hope is found in the Mormon doctrine that provides for marriage sealings after death. Since earthly life in Mormon belief blends smoothly into the hereafter, Mormon singles are constantly assured that they will be married eventually; if they stick it out here, right will be done in the next life.

Work for the dead

The heavy emphasis on priesthood authority perplexes and offends some non-Mormons. Do you mean to say, they will ask, that only Mormon baptisms and Mormon marriages are recognized in heaven? That seems to carry exclusivity to an extreme. Mormons believe that only they have an authorized priesthood and only ordinances performed by that priesthood are valid in eternity. Where does that leave everyone else? Mormons reply that exclusive authority does not mean exclusive access to heaven. Mormon scriptures speak of the Spirit of Christ reaching all men of whatever persuasion, and of God inspiring religious writings beyond the Bible and the Mormon scriptures. One revelation to Smith said that all they who would have accepted the gospel given a chance will be accepted of God.

Paradoxically, Mormonism in some respects is the most universalistic of Christian faiths. The question of the condition of the millions of souls who were born and died without hearing the name of Christ has plagued Christians for centuries. How can Christ redeem those who know nothing of him, and how can God damn the ignorant? Smith's revelations addressed the issue directly by explaining that people who lived without knowing Christ will yet hear his gospel. Following the passages in the first epistle of Peter (1 Peter 3:19 and 4:6) about Christ visiting the dead after his resurrection, Joseph Smith taught that the gospel will be preached in the afterlife and people given a chance to accept it or not, just as people on earth are.

That provision does not answer the question completely. The Peter passages leave unresolved the question of how the dead can undergo the requisite gospel ordinances such as baptism. When Jesus said, "Except a man be born of the water and the spirit he cannot enter the Kingdom of Heaven" (John 3:5), Mormons believe, he meant it literally. Every believer must be baptized. But if baptism—being born of the water—is required by the Christian gospel, how are the dead to embrace Christ? Furthermore, baptism must be performed under the hands of a person holding divine authority.

The Mormon answer is to make the crucial sacraments available to the deceased through the work of living Latter-day Saints in the temple. Mormons have taken upon themselves responsibility for baptizing and for sealing the marriages of every person who ever lived. They are engaged in a huge worldwide effort to film and digitize every genealogical record in existence. The fact that this work entails billions of names and mountains of records does not intimidate the church. Scores of microfilming teams scour archives all over the world, hundreds of volunteers extract genealogical information, and thousands of temple patrons pass through the ordinances as proxies for the dead. Each time church members go through the temple ceremonies after their initial experience, they do work for someone who has died. Members are baptized, given the gift of the Holy Ghost, endowed, married, and sealed to children on behalf of someone else. All ordinances required of the living are provided by proxy for those who have passed on to the next life. Mormons carry on despite occasional complaints. Jews have objected to baptisms being performed for their dead, disliking the implication that their ancestors converted to Mormonism. In response to the complaints, church leaders stopped proxy work for Jews, unless performed for relatives of Mormon converts.

Why does the church persist in this vast effort despite such objections and the huge expense? The relentless determination to gather the records and perform the ordinances testifies to the Mormon desire to reconcile two conflicting impulses, the wish to be inclusive and a belief in the necessity of sacral priesthood. The requirement of baptism applies to everyone, including the billions of souls who never heard of Christ while on earth. The restoration of priesthood by John the Baptist and Peter, James, and John means the priesthood ordinances are not merely symbols of divine truth but requirements for admission into the kingdom of heaven, just like obtaining an authorized visa for admission to a foreign country. To reconcile their belief in an exclusivist priesthood and an equally strong belief in the necessity of giving everyone a chance, Mormons pay the not inconsiderable price of assembling the genealogical records and doing the ordinance work in their temples.

Joseph Smith saw this vast vicarious enterprise as a fulfillment of Malachi's prophecy that the hearts of the fathers must be turned to the children and the children to the fathers or the world would be wasted at the Second Coming (Malachi 4:6). In Smith's mind, work for the dead, as Mormons call it, accomplished more than giving everyone a chance. It created what he called a "welding link." He felt that the human family must be bonded across the generations. Every child and every parent, every wife and every husband, must be bound to one another, forming a great chain stretching back through time. In Mormon thought, the temples are the place where the work of cross-generational bonding takes place.

It is sometimes said that Mormonism is to Christianity as Christianity is to Judaism. Both Mormonism and Christianity established themselves by reinterpreting a preceding faith. Christianity built on Judaism but emphasized the death and resurrection of Jesus Christ; Mormonism began with Christianity but accepted new revelation through a modern prophet.

Ironically, many of the most distinguishing characteristics of Mormonism are Hebraic. In a sense Mormonism differentiated itself from Christianity by returning to Christianity's roots in the religion of ancient Israel. Joseph Smith claimed to have recovered the Hebrew priesthoods of Aaron and Melchizedek and to have revived the prophetic tradition of Moses and Isaiah. Going back to the rituals of ancient Israel, Smith restored temple worship under the direction of a sacral priesthood. Smith even adapted instructions for ordaining priests in the book of Exodus for portions of Mormon temple rites.

Throughout Smith's life, the Old Testament was a major source of inspiration. His restoration can be thought of as purging the Hellenistic influences in Christianity and reviving the Hebraic. When he undertook to educate his unlearned followers, Smith passed over the classical languages and hired a Jewish instructor to teach them Hebrew. In the end, Joseph Smith's restoration pressed Christianity into an Old Testament mold.

Chapter 5
Cosmology

Visions of the eternities

Many Mormons find Joseph Smith's cosmology the most attractive part of his restoration. His cosmological thought takes the form of a story about the nature of the universe and the long course of the soul's history from before the world existed. Although it was not presented in a systematic philosophical treatise—that was not Smith's way—the story can be pieced together from scattered fragments in his revelations and sermons, along with a few epigrammatic asides in conversations. This kind of material appears most densely in his late sermons and in the additional translations he produced after publication of the Book of Mormon.

The Book of Moses

One of the most fruitful sources of Smith's cosmological thought is found in the Book of Moses, a revelation received in 1830, soon after the publication of the Book of Mormon. The Book of Moses began as an independent revelation that evolved into a retranslation of the Bible. The first portion was a four-page report of a vision purportedly given to Moses, possibly at Sinai, on the eve of writing Genesis. Unlike the Book of Mormon's heavily historical account of Israel in America, the Moses revelation rose immediately to the level of cosmology.

The words of God, which he spake unto Moses at a time when Moses was caught up into an exceedingly high mountain, and he saw God face to face, and he talked with him, and the glory of God was upon Moses (Moses 1:1–2).

The revelation tells of God showing Moses the many worlds he has created, among them the earth on which Moses lived.

After beholding the earth and its inhabitants, Moses poses a cosmological question. He boldly asks God why he made the worlds. What was his purpose? At first God is reticent: He will only explain that he has created worlds without number and for his own good reason. Moses presses the point. Tell me at least, he pleads, about this earth. Finally God explains to his importunate prophet why he has created worlds without number. The answer is the single most influential passage in Mormon cosmology: "For behold this is my work and my glory—to bring to pass the immortality and eternal life of man" (Moses 1:39). The entire universe came down to helping humanity find eternal life.

The Vision of Moses

In June 1830, three months after the publication of the Book of Mormon and organization of the church, Joseph Smith received a revelation that purported to be an account of a vision given to Moses before he wrote the Book of Genesis. Later this revelation was divided into verses like the Bible and incorporated into Joseph Smith's revision of the Bible. The entire vision, consisting of forty-three verses, also tells of Moses' encounter with Satan. After a struggle with evil, Moses sees God and his creations and asks about their meaning.

27. And it came to pass, as the voice was still speaking, Moses cast his eyes and beheld the earth, yea, even all of it; and there

was not a particle of it which he did not behold, discerning it by the Spirit of God.

28. And he beheld also the inhabitants thereof, and there was not a soul which he beheld not; and he discerned them by the Spirit of God; and their numbers were great, even numberless as the sand upon the sea.

29. And he beheld many lands; and each land was called earth, and there were inhabitants on the face thereof.

30. And it came to pass that Moses called upon God, saying: Tell me, I pray thee, why these things are so, and by what thou madest them?

31. And behold, the glory of the Lord was upon Moses, so that Moses stood in the presence of God, and talked with him face to face. And the Lord God said unto Moses: For mine own purposes have I made these things. Here is wisdom and it remaineth in me.

32. And by the word of my power, have I created them, which is mine Only Begotten Son, who is full of grace and truth.

33. And worlds without number have I created; and I also created them for mine own purpose; and by the Son I created them, which is mine Only Begotten.

34. And the first man of all men have I called Adam, which is many.

35. But only an account of this earth, and the inhabitants thereof, give I unto you. For behold, there are many worlds that have passed away by the word of my power. And there are many that now stand, and innumerable are they unto man; but all things are numbered unto me, for they are mine and I know them.

36. And it came to pass that Moses spake unto the Lord, saying: Be merciful unto thy servant, O God, and tell me concerning this earth, and the inhabitants

thereof, and also the heavens, and then thy servant will
be content.

37. And the Lord God spake unto Moses, saying: The heavens,
they are many, and they cannot be numbered unto man; but
they are numbered unto me, for they are mine.

38. And as one earth shall pass away, and the heavens thereof
even so shall another come; and there is no end to my works,
neither to my words.

39. For behold, this is my work and my glory—to bring to pass
the immortality and eternal life of man.

The Book of Moses, *The Pearl of Great Price* (Salt Lake City: Church of Jesus Christ of Latter-day Saints, 1981), Moses 1:27–39.

Rather than standing alone as an independent revelation, Smith's
vision of Moses turned into a preface to Genesis. In succeeding
months, Smith began an extended revision and expansion of the
entire Bible, beginning with familiar material from Genesis. A
Bible reader would recognize the account of the Creation as
coming from Genesis but would note differences. The Creation, for
example, was put in the first person. Instead of "In the beginning
God created the heaven and earth" (Genesis 1:1), Smith's Book of
Moses said, "In the beginning I created the heaven and the earth,"
as if God were telling Moses directly how it happened (Moses 2:1).

From there on, Smith worked through both New and Old
Testaments, smoothing out unclear passages, resolving apparent
conundrums, and occasionally introducing extensive new
materials. The work was a measure of his audacity. Ignorant of
ancient languages and only superficially acquainted with the Bible,
he undertook to improve the most honored and holy book in
Western civilization. He called his work a translation, but he had
no original texts before him as he dictated; he relied entirely on his
inspiration. He wrote not as a scholar but as a prophet, putting his
own revelation up against centuries of scholarship.

After Smith completed his revisions in 1833, he made no serious effort to publish the new translation. He may have realized that an altered Bible would hamper missionary work. Missionaries could better reason from the familiar text than from Smith's version. Rather than publishing the revised Bible as a whole, the modern church has integrated his revisions into footnotes and an appendix in the Latter-day Saint printing of the King James Bible.

For the most part Smith reworked phrases and words in his alterations, but in Genesis he added scores of verses. The most extensive revisions are published as the Book of Moses in *The Pearl of Great Price,* a compilation of Smith's miscellaneous inspired writings that is now considered to be scripture. The Book of Moses consists of eight revised chapters from Genesis, going from Adam down to Noah. The book contains an extensive account of Enoch, a seventh-generation biblical prophet after Adam who is mentioned only briefly in the conventional Genesis but is a massive figure in pseudepigraphic works from the second century BCE when Jewish writers were compiling or creating scores of works written in the name of or about biblical prophets. Indeed, Smith's Enoch, because it expands on the biblical verses about Enoch, has the feel of a modern pseudepigraphic addition to scripture.

The Enoch in Smith's translation builds a holy city of Zion that is carried into heaven. Later Enoch sees the history of the world down to the last times, when another holy city will be built up on earth to meet the New Jerusalem coming down from heaven. At this point, the Enoch story converges with the history of the latter-day church. The Latter-day Saint Zion, the text said, will someday meet the Zion of Enoch, and the two cities will rejoice. "They shall see us; and we will fall upon their necks, and they shall fall upon our necks, and we will kiss each other" (Moses 7:63).

Except for this one connection, the Book of Moses had little direct bearing on Smith or the church when it was first published in 1832 and 1833. It seemed like an exotic fragment out of the distant past designed for the instruction of the Saints. It became more relevant later when succeeding revelations began to expand Smith's radical cosmology.

The Book of Abraham

Another translation came to light in 1835, when the church purchased a group of scrolls excavated from an Egyptian tomb and brought by a touring exhibitor to Kirtland, Ohio. On seeing the scrolls, Smith sensed that they contained the writings of Abraham and urged his followers to purchase them. In 1842, the translation was published in the church newspaper as the Book of Abraham.

7. Facsimile no. 1 from the scrolls of the Book of Abraham.

Knowing no Egyptian, Smith once again relied on inspiration for the text. In all of these works, the word *translation* applies only insofar as it suggests Smith was bringing forward the thoughts or revelations of ancient people—Abraham, Moses, and the Book of Mormon prophets—into the modern world. He himself seemed to believe that the words he dictated corresponded to words on the plates or the scrolls, but there is no evidence that he understood the language in the standard linguistic sense.

Joseph Smith published four chapters of Abraham's writings along with three illustrations copied from the scrolls. They told of Abraham's origins in the land of Ur, his struggles with false priests, his journey with his wife into Egypt, his astronomical teachings, and finally an account of the Creation that generally followed Moses' Genesis but differed in significant detail.

Smith's claims to be translating came under criticism in 1966, when fragments of the Abrahamic scrolls, lost in the confusion following his death, were discovered in the Metropolitan Museum of Art in New York City. Modern Egyptologists immediately set to work on the scrolls and found nothing remotely like Smith's Book of Abraham. They were a conventional "breathing permit," a common document (called *sen-sen* in Egyptian) issued to an Egyptian notable at death to help him live in the afterlife. Critics of Smith's fabulous stories immediately felt vindicated, while orthodox Mormons had to reconsider the nature of his translations.

Translation of the scrolls brought the idea of a close correspondence between the Egyptian text and the translated book into question. Some Mormon scholars maintained that since only scraps were found at the Metropolitan Museum, the actual Abraham text had not yet been recovered; others theorized that the scrolls were an occasion for a revelation about Abraham rather than actual writings by the ancient patriarch. More significant than the translation process, they said, were the similarities between Smith's Abraham and the many pseudepigraphic writings about the patriarch that had come down from antiquity. Although unfamiliar with any of these ancient texts at the time, Smith presented themes and stories resembling the ancient Abrahamic literature.

Even more than Smith's Book of Moses, the Book of Abraham (also included in *The Pearl of Great Price*) discoursed on the starry heavens and man's primal encounter with God. Smith published the four chapters in Nauvoo in 1842 during his most fecund period of cosmological teaching. For the past few years, he had been touching on ideas about the nature of the human intelligence and the meaning of Creation. These observations from his sermons, added to the writings of Moses and Abraham, created a rich if unordered mixture of cosmological thought.

Stories of eternity

Three months before his death, Smith brought together the themes running through his writings in a long sermon now called the King Follett discourse, named for a man whose death was the occasion for the preaching. The sermon, one of the most startling and heterodox of the nineteenth century, made clear how far Smith had departed from conventional Christian theology of his time. He had created a new story of the Creation and the destiny of humankind.

The departures begin with Creation. Smith did not conceive of Creation as *ex nihilo*, with the universe suddenly appearing by divine fiat out of nothing in a single big bang. In his thought, there never was a time of utter nothingness. Smith taught that "the elements are eternal" and coexist eternally with God (Doctrine and Covenants 93:33). God did not create matter; it was always there. He organized it. The Book of Abraham said the Gods "organized and formed the heavens and the earth" (Abraham 4:1). Creation was more like bringing order out of chaos than making something out of nothing. In the King Follett discourse Smith explained that Creation was the "same as you would organize a Ship" from available materials.[1] Creation could be thought of as God moving through an unorganized and chaotic universe and establishing order. In the Book of Moses, Enoch comments that God has created millions of worlds, one at a time, through the eons of eternity.

To the eternity of matter, Smith's revelations added the eternity of the soul. Intelligence was not created any more than matter was, an early revelation announced. "Man was also in the beginning with God. Intelligence, or the light of truth, was not created or made, neither indeed can be" (Doctrine and Covenants 93:29). Mormons differ among themselves about the form of man "in the beginning." Were we distinct personalities or merely part of a great soup of intelligence? Whatever the exact form, Joseph Smith's intention clearly was to assert that some essence of the human personality, like matter itself, has always been. God used this pre-existing intelligence to create spirit beings. In the King Follett discourse, Smith affirmed that God is a self-existing being but goes on to declare that "man exhists upon the same principle.... The spirit of man ... does not have a beginning or end.... God never had power to create the spirit of man [just as] God himself could not create himself. Intelligence is eternal and it is self-exhisting."[2]

According to the Book of Abraham, these primal intelligences were ranked up and down in a hierarchy. The Lord tells Abraham:

> These two facts do exist, that there are two spirits, one being more intelligent than the other; there shall be another more intelligent than they; I am the Lord thy God, I am more intelligent than they all (Abraham 3:19).

The passage evoked the classic image of the great chain of being with God at the pinnacle and other intelligences, perhaps including animals and plants, extending below him. Earthly race and class did not enter into this configuration, only intelligence.

Smith pictured a moment when God came down among these intelligences and offered to instruct them. As he said in the 1844 King Follett discourse, God finding "himself in the midst of spirit and glory because he was greater saw proper to institute laws whereby the rest could have a privilege to advance like himself." God did not present himself as sovereign but as teacher and father, offering to help the intelligences grow. The goal of their growth was to become like him—gods themselves in some sense. "God has power to institute laws to instruct the weaker intelligences that thay may be exhalted with himself" into a godly order.[3] He did not dominate them but nurtured them as a father. As he explained to Moses: "This is my work and my glory—to bring to pass the immortality and eternal life of man" (Moses 1:39).

This story of the beginning envisions a profoundly voluntaristic universe. Human beings are not the creatures of God, because he did not create their inner essence. They are radically free intelligences, as eternal as God himself. Nor did he impose his will on these lesser intelligences through an exercise of power. He offered them laws by which they could advance with the option of accepting or not. The books of Abraham and Moses incorporate this choice into a story. They tell about a time when Lucifer, a brilliant spirit in the heavenly realms, offered "to redeem all mankind, that one soul shall not be lost" (Moses 4:1). The drawback of this guaranteed salvation was that Lucifer would destroy human agency. All would be compelled to be saved. Following God and Christ entailed the huge risk of sin and suffering. By allowing spirits their freedom, God left room for some to fall out of his presence into the realms of darkness and chaos. Although Lucifer was slated to became Satan, his promise of assured salvation was sufficiently attractive that a third of the hosts of heaven followed him. All the spirits who came to earth chose to take the risk.

In this cosmology, God does not dominate existence as the conventional Christian God does. He does not make the world out of nothing; he does not make human intelligence; he does not impose his law on his subjects. He invites them to join him in seeking the fullness of existence which he himself enjoys.

Smith's theology did not simplify the universe as conventional Christian theology does. Traditionally, God is the all-encompassing being that makes and comprehends everything; the universe is essentially unitary, a manifestation of a single divine mind. Smith's universe, filled with loads of unorganized matter, all manner of independent intelligences, and millions of earths, is profoundly pluralistic, made up of lots of things. God advances through the realms of unorganized matter, bringing order to this pluralistic universe, but not everything can be reduced to his mind and will.

Smith did not see this God as having always been in power as God. In a profoundly evolving universe, where change is always occurring, where some intelligences are advancing while others head off on their own under a lesser being, God himself learned to be divine. At the far edge of his theological speculations, Smith argued in the King Follett discourse that God once was a man and had a father like everyone else. He lived on an earth and was taught and advanced under the tutelage of a preceding God. In a few sentences, Smith postulated an alliance of divine beings stretching back in time and outward in space, working together to bring along lesser spirits to become divine beings—a process that never began and will never end.

Critics charge Mormons with believing in multiple gods, but the Mormon God is as unified as the trinity of Christian theology. These Gods do not contend with one another like the gods in the pagan pantheon. They have agreed on the same principles and work for the same end. They are one as Christ and the Father are one. God invites humans to join in this grand alliance, much as Christ prayed that his disciples would be one in him as he is one with the Father (John 17:21).

Cosmology and the conduct of life

Mormons think only infrequently of the complex universe and
the great alliance of the Gods going back in time. The part of the
story that Mormons refer to most is the moment in their spirits'
history when God offered to send them to earth and they
accepted his plan. For Mormons, this decision, more than the
fall of Adam and Eve, is the backdrop for earthly life. They are less
concerned about the burden of original sin, which they believe
Christ has totally overcome for everyone, than whether they can
meet the test they were sent to earth to face. Having taken a
chance on freedom away from God's presence and with their
memories of heaven blanked out, will they choose the right?
They feel the temptations of the flesh and the allure of worldly
pride and want to prove they can choose godliness over
worldliness. They do not blame the Fall for the evil in their hearts;
it is their own perversity and the evil influences in the earth
that trouble them. They pray to God the Father in the name of
Christ, asking for help to live good lives during their time on earth.

How well they are doing can never be known for sure. Many
Mormons have doubts about where they stand with God. On the
one hand, they speak confidently of being with their families in
heaven and enjoying the presence of the Heavenly Father. On
the other hand, few will assert positively that they feel worthy
of the high degree of exaltation promised in Mormon theology—
becoming like God. They know their Father-God wants everyone
to become like him, but he is a being of perfect holiness and glory.
Humans cannot enter his presence without being pure and
righteous; all fall short. Humanity in Mormonism, as in all
Christian thought, is blighted with sin.

The Mormon understanding of heaven complicates this
self-evaluation. One of Joseph Smith's revelations spoke of
three heavens or degrees of glory—telestial, terrestrial, and

celestial—each with a different degree of access to God. Most of humanity will inherit one of these kingdoms in the afterlife, Smith was told, alleviating tremendously the fear of hell. Standard Christian theology sharply divided the afterworld into heaven and hell, with much of humanity in danger of condemnation. Smith's revelation informed him that only those who had known the power of God in this life and rejected it, a very small group known as the Sons of Perdition, will ultimately be cast into hell.

All the rest, including the worst sinners, will be redeemed. The "liars, and sorcerers, and adulterers, and whoremongers, and whosoever loves and makes a lie," will suffer the wrath of God until the last day and then be resurrected and assigned to one of the realms of glory (Doctrine and Covenants 76:103). The blackest sinners will inhabit the telestial kingdom while people of greater virtue will dwell in the terrestrial and the celestial kingdoms. All will enjoy a degree of glory. The consequences of horrible sins are eternal but not devastating.

This picture of heaven relieves Mormons' concerns about hell. They care more about rising to the highest degree of glory in the celestial kingdom than keeping out of the devil's clutches. Smith's vision described inhabitants of the kingdom just below the celestial—the terrestrial—as ones who were not valiant in the testimony of Jesus. Mormons fear that they are not valiant enough for the celestial kingdom. Thus the intense activity, the striving, the self-examination, and sometimes the resignation found in Mormon spiritual life.

In recent years, Mormons have talked more about the grace of Christ. Nineteenth-century Mormonism defined itself against Calvinistic religions. The Calvinist assertion of human incapacity and utter dependence on grace seemed to early Mormons like a distortion of Jesus' message. In reaction, Mormon preachers and writers emphasized good works and moral obligation, the gospel of James rather than Paul. Late-twentieth-century Mormonism pulled back from this entrenched aversion to doctrines of grace. Mormons have rediscovered the grace passages in the Book of Mormon and lean on them for reassurance about their standing before God, learning to trust in Christ while doing their best to do good works.

They are learning that when examined closely, Joseph Smith's story of eternity underscores the necessity of the atonement in the great plan of God. It is no small thing that vicious sinners are eventually saved into one of the kingdoms of glory. The great earth venture of the spirits who accepted God's plan could have become a horrible tragedy. In offering a program that called for individual intelligences to enter a realm of moral freedom on earth, God risked the loss of many of his children. Billions of souls might fail to return and perhaps be worse off than when they began. A third of the hosts of heaven went with Lucifer at the beginning; more might fall away in the duress of earth life.

What prevents this tragedy from occurring is the atonement of Jesus Christ. Jesus was crucified to bear the sins of all the lost and wayward spirits making their way through the world. He saves all but those who crucify him unto themselves by rejecting him after they have known his godly power. His sacrifice brings even the vicious and the rebellious out of hell. Through Christ, all those who agreed to the plan achieve some degree of glory in the end. Christ has indeed conquered death and hell.

For those whose sins are less serious, as Mormons are beginning to see, the atonement is no less critical. Their aspirations are very high. They seek to become gods themselves, an impossibly demanding standard. How can they expect to rise to such heights? Their own scriptures tell them their only hope is in "Jesus the mediator of the new covenant, who wrought out this perfect atonement through the shedding of his own blood" (Doctrine and Covenants 76:69). Even the most righteous can only come to God through Christ.

The Mormon outlook

Informed by these stories of eternity, Mormons look at life in a variety of interrelated ways. They see it as a test of their ability to cleave to God in the face of worldly temptations. Will they be worthy to return to the God who sent them here? They also embrace earth life as an opportunity to obtain a body and learn the difference between good and evil. Earth is a school for learning how to choose the good while embodied in flesh, which is considered a necessity for attaining the highest joy. Finally, Momons see earth life as a time to bind themselves to God and Christ through covenants that make them part of the grand alliance of beings who have found the way to godhood.

These covenants come in varying forms, from baptism and the sacrament of the Lord's Supper through accepting the priesthood and marrying for eternity. In a sense the various covenants are all variants of the fundamental covenant that God made with Abraham: I will be your God and you will be my people, and through you I will bless the people of the earth. They all bind people to God with ever more secure bonds, to the end that his children may receive a fullness of his glory and in effect enjoy the life of God.

The sacrament prayer said each Sunday before the distribution of the Lord's Supper lays out specifically the terms of one of these covenants. The prayer says that by eating of the bread, the communicants take upon themselves the name of the Son, and pledge always to remember him and keep his commandments, which he has given them. In return, the communicants are promised that his Spirit, meaning the Spirit of Christ, will always be with them. This is no small matter, because the Spirit of Christ is the light that radiates from God to fill the immensity of space and uphold all of creation. It is the light that enlightens the eye and the light that

Blessing on the Bread

Latter-day Saints partake of the Lord's Supper weekly. Two priesthood holders, often young priests between the ages of sixteen and eighteen, break the bread into small pieces and then offer this prayer. A similar prayer is offered over the water. Deacons, usually ages twelve and thirteen, pass the bread and water along the pews in trays so that everyone can partake.

O God, the Eternal Father, we ask thee in the name of thy Son, Jesus Christ, to bless and sanctify this bread to the souls of all those who partake of it, that they may eat in remembrance of the body of thy Son, and witness unto thee, O God, the Eternal Father, that they are willing to take upon them the name of thy Son, and always remember him and keep his commandments which he has given them; that they may always have his Spirit to be with them. Amen.

The Doctrine and Covenants of the Church of Jesus Christ of Latter-day Saints (Salt Lake City: Church of Jesus Christ of Latter-day Saints, 1981), 20:77.

enlightens the understanding. "The glory of God is intelligence," another scripture says, and this great light-intelligence can flow into humble communicants through the covenant in the sacrament prayer (Doctrine and Covenants 93:36). Intelligence is not capped in any individual human. It can grow and expand through diligence, obedience, and remembrance of Christ. All that is encompassed in the prayer on the Lord's Supper.

Probably few Latter-day Saints contemplate the complexities of this elaborate world picture very often, but it shapes the Mormon attitude toward life on earth. Primarily it locates Latter-day Saints in a friendly universe, governed by a God whose work and glory it is to bring them to immortality and eternal life. He is a God who wishes to share his fullness with them, wants to instruct them in how to become like him, and has provided a Savior through whom they can escape the horrible consequences of their sins.

When bad things happen, Latter-day Saints are not likely to blame God. They realize that they and everyone else in the world are radically free to do both good and evil, and bad things will result from pure human wickedness. Though God does intervene in history, Mormons realize that he may not protect them from every evil. He will help them, however, to turn evil into good and bring some measure of redemption out of the worst disasters. They do not complain that by rights a just God should have designed the world to protect the innocent from their terrible sufferings. Mormons believe that perfect control, Satan's plan, would have ended human agency. Although he does not eradicate every evil through exercise of his immense power, the Mormon God works with his children to overcome the world's wrongs.

Some observers say Mormons lack a sense of the tragic. They are too optimistic, so the critique goes, and fail to grasp the despair that envelops so many of the world's people. The tragic is certainly present in Mormon theology and history: The thousand-year-old Nephite civilization in the Book of Mormon perished because of pride and hard-heartedness; a third of the hosts of heaven turned from God into darkness; the Mormon people have been persecuted and driven. But rather than taking these as evidence of the essential tragedy of human history, Mormons remember their friendly Father in heaven and the promise of eternal life. They are not borne down by the setbacks in their own history, the recurring persecutions and the terrible mistakes. They read existence as a divine comedy with a happy ending always in sight. Their resolve is not easily broken.

It was, in fact, their inveterate confidence that enabled the Mormons to transport the church across the desolate high plains of North America and plant their communities in the forbidding environment of the Great Basin.

Chapter 6
Nineteenth-century Utah

Succession

When Joseph Smith died in June 1844, he left no clear line of
succession—or rather he left too many potential successors. He had
taken great pride in the councils he had organized to manage
various units of the church, foremost among them the Quorum
of the Twelve Apostles, whose senior member at the time of
his death was Brigham Young. In the succession controversy in
the summer of 1844, Young put forward the case for the Twelve
Apostles, with himself as their head, to lead the church—a kind
of Peter of the latter days.

Besides commissioning the Twelve, Smith had spoken of
priesthood descending through family lines, and he was said to
have given blessings to his son Joseph Smith III promising him a
leading role. In addition, Joseph Smith's longtime colleague and
unwavering counselor in the First Presidency, Sidney Rigdon,
aspired to succeed the Prophet. At a public meeting in Nauvoo
on August 8, 1844, two months after Smith's death, Rigdon
made his case for his right to lead as former counselor to the
Prophet. Rigdon spoke for an hour and a half in the morning,
and that afternoon Brigham Young spoke for himself and the
Twelve. Young claimed that Smith had conferred the governing
priesthood authority on the Twelve Apostles. When the

congregation was asked to vote, they raised their hands for the Apostles. A month later Rigdon was still asserting his superiority to the Twelve and was excommunicated. The following spring he organized his own church with its own apostles and prophet. Ignoring his other rivals, Young took charge of the main body of the church as it prepared for its western exodus.

8. Brigham Young, 1851.

Although Young asserted his authority over the most coherent group of Mormons at the time, the succession question remained alive. Large numbers of Smith's followers did not accept Young and the Twelve as the legitimate heirs to Joseph Smith. A variety of claims arose in Smith's wake, the most successful initially being that of James J. Strang, a recent convert to Mormonism who reported revelations and opened a colony on Beaver Island in Lake Michigan. Strang gathered a surprising number of onetime Mormons to his fold before, going from excess to excess, he was shot to death by two disillusioned followers, and his church collapsed.

Subsequently, the most successful attempt to form an alternative to Young and the Utah Mormons was the Reorganized Church of Jesus Christ of Latter Day Saints (RLDS) formed in the late 1850s. This movement sprang up among scattered Mormons who chose not to go west but still desired the spiritual satisfactions of Smith's restoration. The organizers of this movement, led by Jason W. Briggs and Zenos H. Gurley, eventually persuaded Joseph Smith III to acknowledge his legacy as the Prophet's firstborn and take the presidency. Along with her son, Emma Smith, now married to Lewis Bidamon, joined the movement.

Always smaller and milder than the Utah Mormons, the Reorganized Church offered an alternative version of Joseph Smith's restoration for the thousands of Mormons who were uneasy with plural marriage, temple rites, and Brigham Young. To the end of the century, the Utah leadership worried about the claims of Joseph's firstborn to the church presidency. The RLDS Church claims were strong enough to win court cases over legal succession, giving them control of major Mormon sites such as the temple in Kirtland and Smith's property in Nauvoo. The RLDS eventually made Independence, Missouri, the original Zion, its headquarters and established a presence in the Midwest. For a century and a half, a direct descendant of Joseph Smith governed the RLDS Church until precedent was broken in 1996, when a leader was chosen on the basis of experience and competence rather than descent.

Migration

After Smith's death, the Nauvoo Saints under Brigham Young hoped for a respite from the persecution that had plagued them while Smith lived. He had been the target of the most intense opposition; would his removal dissipate the enmity? To the Mormons' dismay, the anger and fear only increased. In the fall of 1845, the governor of Illinois informed Young that the Mormons had to go or be exposed to further vigilante attacks. The body of Mormons was still large enough to control many county offices, and the same individuals who had directed their fire against Smith now turned on the Mormons as a whole. When their enemies burned two hundred houses and barns, the Mormons saw they must leave. By January 1845, Young was planning an exodus beyond the borders of the United States to a yet undetermined destination. Texas, Upper California, and Oregon were all given consideration. Gradually Upper California emerged as the most suitable site for a Mormon colony.

The first contingent of Mormons left Nauvoo when trails to the West were not yet open and before the grass for cattle was growing. After frantic preparations for departure in the fall and winter, Young led the first party across the Mississippi on February 4, 1846. For the next three months a pitiful string of Mormon wagons worked its way across Iowa to the Missouri River, where they built winter quarters and gathered their forces for a year before continuing the journey to Utah. In July 1847, after a 1,300-mile journey, Brigham Young led the first party of Mormons into the Salt Lake Valley, where he established headquarters for the migrants who were to follow.

Through the nineteenth century, Utah was the destination of more than eighty thousand Mormons who migrated from their homelands in the eastern United States and Europe to the new Zion. Brigham Young became an expert colonizer, famed in American history. He planted hundreds of settlements from Idaho to Arizona and as far away as California. Accustomed to thinking of themselves as a society, the Mormons combined civic and ecclesiastical organizations to keep the peace, build irrigation canals, regulate water distribution, organize schools, and handle every aspect of civil government. Well before the United States established a territorial government, the Mormons, building on the tradition of the City of Zion, set up all the necessary institutions of civic life in a smooth blend of church and state.

Legacy

These pioneering years had far less impact on Mormonism than the immensely creative period of the founding under Joseph Smith. Modern Mormons still reach back to Smith's revelations to authenticate their beliefs and practices. No church leader since Smith has shaped Mormon culture so definitively. But Brigham Young and his successors in nineteenth-century Utah left their mark. Mormons still call upon memories of Young's achievements to define themselves in the twenty-first century. Because the pioneer period tested Mormon mettle, Mormons tap the nineteenth century less for doctrine than for the definition of their character.

To this day, Mormons celebrate the 24th of July, the day Brigham Young arrived in the valley, as a Mormon festival on a par with the 4th of July. The pioneer period stands alongside the restoration of the gospel by Joseph Smith as a key episode in the heroic era of Latter-day Saint history. The oft-repeated stories of the westward trek inspire modern Mormons to develop pioneer virtues themselves. To dramatize the early Mormons' heroics, young Mormons go on "treks" during which they live a few days under pioneer conditions, sometimes pulling handcarts across difficult terrain in imitation of their forefathers' hardships. Children sing a song about the handcart pioneers having to "walk and walk and walk and walk." Pioneer suffering and courage are reminders of the obligation to carry on the faith under the hardships and trials of modern times. Converts across the world are absorbed into the pioneer epic. They are depicted as modern pioneers whose difficult journey was to join the church and establish Zion in their own countries. The pioneer story is meant to imbue the coming generations with a resolve not to betray their heritage.

Plural marriage

The practice of plural marriage, the single best known feature of Mormonism in the nineteenth century and even now, is far more difficult to assimilate into modern Mormons' self-understanding. It clashes with the church's emphasis on perfect loyalty between husband and wife and eternal companionship. Mormons have trouble explaining to themselves why the practice was instituted. Many put the doctrine on the shelf, hoping they can understand it later.

Plural marriage also raises questions about Joseph Smith. What were his motives? Mormons believe a revelation commanded him to take additional wives, but the lurid accounts by non-Mormon critics throw his character into question. Did his libido affect his judgment? Mormons are most concerned about Smith's relationship with his wife Emma, a woman he apparently loved deeply. Why did he hide his other marriages from her for so long? He seemed to sacrifice his relationship with his wife to comply with his revelation.

Joseph Smith instituted plural marriage secretly in Nauvoo in the 1840s, but by the time the Saints had established their beachhead in Utah, its existence was common knowledge. The practice was publicly announced at a church general conference in 1852. Smith had married his first plural wife in the early 1830s in response to a revelation he apparently received in 1831 but said nothing about for a decade. In 1841, he began to marry additional women until the number grew to more than thirty. (Incomplete records make it impossible to determine an exact number.) Smith probably understood the explosive nature of this new revelation and seems to have resisted complying himself. In 1843, in an effort to persuade his resistant first wife, Emma, he dictated a transcription of the words he claims to have received.

The revelation offered no rationale for plural marriage satisfactory to modern understanding. The chief justification was that Abraham and the ancient patriarchs had several wives, and Joseph and the church were to follow their lead as part of the restoration of all things. Smith had turned to the Hebrew Bible for the temple and priesthood; now that same search yielded plural marriage. The Book of Mormon, in a passage condemning men for taking concubines, added a little insight. Almost tangentially, it commented that monogamy was the divine standard unless God "will raise up seed unto me." Only then would he command his people, as if plural marriage were instituted by the Lord from time to time when he wished to create a new people (Jacob 2:30).

Critics accused Smith of indulging his lusts and exercising his authority to create a harem for his own pleasure. That image does not comport with the way he went about the practice. He usually approached the relatives of his potential wives to seek permission. He did not romance women in order to persuade them but explained doctrine: They and their families would be blessed eternally if the woman would agree to marry the Prophet. If she concurred, the pair was formally married in a ceremony with witnesses. Although there is clear evidence that some sexual relations were involved, Smith did not set up a harem. The extent of his relationships with his plural wives is unclear; he could not have seen them frequently and still kept the fact hidden from Emma. No indisputable offspring resulted from the marriages, in contrast to her frequent pregnancies. DNA tests of purported male descendants have yielded only negative results.

Except in a few instances of women already residing in his household, Smith did not take his plural wives into his home. After marriage, the women returned to live with their families, and he spent little time with them. He seems to have been motivated by a passion to be bound to people more than to indulge his sexual desires. In the same period, orphans and other children were sealed to him as their father. One passage in the marriage revelation promised that God would give him "an hundredfold in this world, of fathers and mothers, brothers and sisters, houses and lands, wives and children, and crowns of eternal lives in the eternal worlds" (Doctrine and Covenants 132:55).

Plural marriage reached its peak in the decade after its announcement in 1852. In the decennial federal censuses, the highest percentage of the population in polygamous families was in 1860: 43.6 percent. After that the number of plural marriages declined until only 25 percent of the population was in polygamous families in 1880 and 7.1 percent in 1900. The main reason for marrying plurally was religious. The plural marriage rate shot up when church leaders emphasized the principle and declined as the preaching relaxed. The 1850s, a period of religious reformation in Utah, produced many plural marriages. If asked why they entered these relationships, both plural wives and husbands emphasized the spiritual blessings of being sealed eternally and of submitting to God's will.

Besides the doctrinal reasons, the practice made some economic sense. The close study of the marriages in one nineteenth-century Utah community revealed that a disproportionate number of plural wives were women who arrived in Utah without fathers or brothers to care for them. As immigration surged, so did plural marriages, integrating single women without other support into the society. Since better-off men more frequently married plurally, the practice distributed wealth to the poor and disconnected. Most of these polygamous families included only two wives at one time, though other wives may have been attached to the husband before

9. Ira Eldredge (1810–1866) and his three wives, Nancy Black Eldredge (1812–1895), Hannah Mariah Savage Eldredge (1832–1905), and Helvig Marie Anderson Eldredge (1844–1939).

death or divorce. Men with higher ecclesiastical standing had three wives at a time on average.

The church renounced plural marriage in 1890 as a necessary condition for Utah to achieve statehood. It had been long denied—when the state was otherwise qualified—because of objections to the practice. The Manifesto, as the announcement by church president Wilford Woodruff was called, did not repudiate polygamy as a principle but declared only that no more plural marriages were being performed. The original plural marriage revelation is still included in the canon of Latter-day Saint scripture. The reason is that the revelation also contains the doctrine of eternal marriage, one of the preeminent tenets of contemporary Mormonism. Besides commanding Smith to take additional wives, the marriage revelation taught that marriages performed by the priesthood would last forever. Moreover, men and women could not reach the highest realms of heavenly glory unless bound to each other as husband and wife. If they were "sealed," their union would last eternally, including the capacity for offspring. The highest condition humans could achieve was to be bound into eternal families.

What carried over from the nineteenth century, then, was celestial or eternal marriage minus the plurality of wives. The doctrine of eternal bonding remains, but without the obligation to take more wives. Mormons believe that the commitment for eternity strengthens marriage in this life. In practice a temple marriage is no guarantee of perfect bliss, nor does it prevent divorce. Temple-married couples can divorce civilly, freeing them to remarry, and with difficulty can be unsealed eternally, but the percentage of divorce is far lower than among the married population as a whole, partly, no doubt, the result of the common values the partners share. The idea of an eternal marriage also motivates the couple to make the marriage work.

10. Large crowds celebrate the laying of the capstone of the Salt Lake Temple in 1892. The temple took forty years to build.

After 1890, some Mormons resolved to continue what they called "the principle" despite the instruction of the First Presidency, wanting to retain both marriage for eternity and plurality of wives. These "fundamentalists" fractured into various sects that continue polygamy to this day. They believe that the church administration erred in abandoning a fundamental of Mormonism. To their way of thinking, the church buckled under pressure. Some claim that their founder received a special commission from an earlier church president, John Taylor, to keep the faith after the rest of the church went astray. Although they comprise a tiny fraction of all the kinds of Mormons, they generate press far out of proportion to their numbers. Some attempt to remain within the fold of the mother church in the belief that the temple rites still are valid. The church repudiates these groups and excommunicates their members if discovered.

Although the marriage revelation still stands among the church's canonized scriptures, neither leaders nor lay Mormons show any disposition to return to polygamy. Mormons think of nineteenth-century plural marriage as a test of devotion, one they might not pass themselves. They honor their polygamous ancestors but admire them from afar. Plural marriage is chiefly experienced as a burden in their relations with non-Mormons. The most common response to news that a fellow worker is a Mormon is the good-hearted jibe "How many wives do you have?" Mormons quickly disabuse the inquirers about plural marriage today and marvel that the old idea has survived for more than a century after polygamy was ended.

Women of Mormondom

The practice of plural marriage had a strangely contradictory effect on women in nineteenth-century Utah. In popular mythology, the plural wife was browbeaten, repressed, and backward, the victim of her patriarchal husband's dominant desires. And Mormon women did complain about having to share their husbands, thinking of a relationship more in keeping with the romantic ideal. Husbands sometimes distanced themselves from their wives and failed to give each one adequate attention. Many women suffered from poverty in a lean economy with many mouths to feed.

Yet Mormon women did not disappear into meek obscurity. With Brigham Young's encouragement, they asserted themselves in politics and the economy. The national critics of plural marriage thought that one solution to polygamy was to give Utah women the vote; once enfranchised, it was assumed, they would remove all pro-polygamy officeholders. But that prediction proved to be unfounded. Mormon women conducted public rallies in support of plural marriage. Whatever sufferings they may have undergone or complaints they secretly harbored, Mormon women publicly supported the principle. Confident of their backing, the Utah territorial legislature granted them the franchise in 1870, second only to the women of Wyoming. While most other women were still campaigning for this recognition, Mormon women were voting until the federal government took away the right in 1887.

Emboldened by their privileges in Utah, Mormon women enthusiastically joined the campaign for national woman suffrage. They were recognized by national suffrage leaders as among the most advanced women in the country. With the blessing of Brigham Young, Mormon women founded a journal, the *Woman's Exponent,* in which they voiced their opinions on every issue of the day—though they remained unfailingly loyal to church leadership.

Modern Mormon women who had largely forgotten this legacy rediscovered the *Woman's Exponent* in the 1970s and recognized kindred spirits in this previous generation. The modern women revived the nineteenth-century journal, calling it *Exponent II,* again with a basic loyalty to the church and its doctrine but committed to exploring the role of women in Mormondom. They used the example of their nineteenth-century ancestors to negotiate their relationship with the feminist movement of the late twentieth century. Unlike Catholic and Protestant women, few Mormons campaigned for ordination to the priesthood, which would have given them access to the higher positions of church leadership. They knew from everyday experience that women had plenty of responsibility in the lay-run congregations where there were rarely enough men and women to perform all the necessary tasks. Women preached and prayed in church, they taught classes, and they had a limited but consistent place in congregational leadership councils. What Mormon women wanted, as measured by the writings in *Exponent II,* was a voice. They wanted to count when decisions were made, and they insisted that attention be paid to the peculiar problems of young mothers, single women, abused women, and others in need of help.

These modern women looked to their nineteenth-century predecessors for models in claiming a larger part in church affairs. Pioneer women had exerted their influence through the Relief Society, an organization Joseph Smith had authorized in Nauvoo in 1842 with Emma Smith as president. As its name indicates, the Relief Society had a primary mission, like so many other ladies' organizations of the day, to succor those in need. In particular the Mormon women were concerned about clothing the workers building the Nauvoo temple. Smith gave them a broad charge to function as a women's version of the priesthood, ministering to all kinds of needs, including the moral rectitude of the Saints.

Brigham Young did not reinstate the Relief Society in Utah until 1867, when he brought it back into existence as part of his campaign to bolster the Utah economy. Through the Relief Society, women cultivated silkworms and spun thread for dresses, contributing to Young's program to make the Utah economy self-sufficient. The Relief Society women encouraged home industries and stored food in preparation for the periodic plagues of locusts that destroyed the crops. Young urged women to take their places behind the counters and keep the books of

Utah businesses in order to increase their productive labor. Twentieth-century Mormon women drew inspiration from their nineteenth-century foremothers' expansive roles in the state's economy and politics and claimed a broader sphere of action for themselves.

It is probably safe to say that on the whole Mormon women believe that their most significant role is in the home as nurturers of the next generation. During the feminist movement of the second half of the twentieth century, church leaders opposed the view that women could be fulfilled only outside the home, and Mormon women largely concurred. Most Mormon women think of marriage and children as the life they most desire. But single women, mothers whose children have been raised or who have lost husbands, and women who feel restive if confined strictly to the home pursue work and careers. Mormon women typically remain at home when their children are young, but many cultivate careers before and after that time—with church encouragement.

The campaign against theocracy

Mormon memory is selective in what it recalls about the church's nineteenth-century history. Mormons have forgotten or actively suppressed parts of that history. The forty-year battle between the church and the U.S. government in the nineteenth century seems at odds with the enthusiastic patriotism of the Mormon heartland today. That struggle is remembered now as one more example of a beleaguered people fighting for liberty to follow their conscience. But the details are glossed over because of the ambivalence about a fight that centered on polygamy. Their ancestors fought for a cause that no longer stirs contemporary Mormons. As a result, the long political struggle, like polygamy itself, is largely ignored.

At the time, the issues were too pronounced to be long forgotten. The Protestant establishment in the United States considered plural marriage an unpardonable offense against Christian morality and civilized behavior. Republican campaign literature linked polygamy with slavery as one of the "twin relics of barbarism." The horror at polygamy along with rumors of Brigham Young's theocratic rule in Utah fueled a campaign against Mormonism that lasted for the entire second half of the nineteenth century. Appalling stories of Brigham Young's one-man rule in Utah convinced officials in Washington that there would be no justice until this proto-tyrant was replaced with federally appointed territorial officials.

In 1857, the conflict grew so heated that President James Buchanan sent an army to Utah to wrest power from the hands of Brigham Young. News of its approach terrified Mormons. For more than two decades they had been harassed, stripped of property, and driven from their homes by persecuting mobs, without any protection from local or national authorities. The Mormons had moved west in hopes of escaping further persecution. In 1857, the arduous trek to Utah appeared to have been made in vain. The United States dispatched troops to dominate them again, and there was nowhere else to go. Brigham Young ordered Mormons in the northern, more settled portions of the state to migrate south and then sent Mormon military parties east along the trail to harass the approaching troops. The Mormons piled straw against the buildings in Salt Lake City and were ready to set them ablaze if the troops invaded.

In this incendiary environment, the greatest tragedy of Mormon history occurred. On September 11, 1857, in a tiny community far to the south, Mormons slaughtered around 120 non-Mormon immigrants at a place called Mountain Meadows near Cedar City, Utah. The migrants' train, made up largely of a party from Arkansas along with a few Missourians, all headed for California, had annoyed Mormons and Indians along the road coming south from Salt Lake City but had done nothing to provoke so violent a reaction.

When a few of the migrants got drunk, threatened the Mormons, and derided Joseph Smith in Cedar City, the local church and militia leaders invited the Indians to run off the immigrants' cattle and give them a scare. The situation got out of hand when an overzealous Mormon named John D. Lee, a federal appointee overseeing the Indians, fired on the train and a full-scale Indian onslaught ensued. When word leaked out that the Mormons were involved in the attack, militia and church leaders, probably fearful of the consequences if their participation were known, decided the party must be destroyed.

The immigrants were holding off the Indians until the Mormons, under the direction of Cedar City ecclesiastical and militia leaders, lured them out with a promise of protection. As they walked unarmed in single file along the trail, the Mormons turned on the immigrants and shot them at close range or clubbed them to death. Those who tried to escape were run down and killed. Seventeen of the youngest children were saved and later placed in Mormon families. Brigham Young has been blamed for ordering this massacre at Mountain Meadows, but he was far too astute not to see the damning effect of such an event on Mormon fortunes. He may have stirred up the local leaders by preaching against the invading army, but no hard evidence that he ordered the massacre has ever been found.

For years efforts were made to locate the perpetrators, but only John D. Lee was ever convicted for the crime. After an initial effort to identify the guilty parties, Brigham Young stopped his inquiries and hushed up the reports. Mormons have no defense for this horrific deed except their fear of invasion, hysteria, and a long history of persecution. Like the men who killed Joseph Smith in 1844, the leaders of the massacre were ordinary, respectable citizens whose humanity broke down at one terrible moment.

For decades Mormons covered up the crime. Mormon children never heard of the event. Church leaders discouraged discussion.

Locals in the vicinity of Mountain Meadows refused to talk about it. Only in recent years has the church openly acknowledged the barbarity of what happened and set up a marker in honor of the migrants. Unfortunately, the Mountain Meadows Massacre fed into the prevalent stereotype of Mormons as fanatics. Even today, critics consider it the archetypical event in Mormon history. Mormons protest in vain. The modest, ordinary lives of millions of Mormons fail to dispel this image of an inherently violent religion.

News of the massacre steeled the resolve of the U.S. Congress to stop polygamy and dissolve Mormon theocracy. In 1862, within a decade of the announcement of Mormon polygamy, Congress passed anti-bigamy legislation targeting Mormons, although for a quarter of a century this legislation did not take hold. Intent on practicing their religion despite federal opposition, Mormons found ways to elude the law. They located jurisdiction over polygamy cases in probate courts, where the territorial legislature rather than federal officials made appointments. To escape anti-bigamy laws, they defined second marriages as sealings rather than marriages, forcing Congress to legislate against cohabitation.

Following a procedure later employed successfully by the civil rights movement, the Mormons submitted cases to test the constitutionality of the anti-bigamy laws. They believed their practice was legal on the grounds of religious freedom guaranteed by the First Amendment to the U.S. Constitution. Their hopes ended in 1879 in the case of *U.S. v. Reynolds,* in which the U.S. Supreme Court declared the anti-bigamy laws to be constitutional. After *Reynolds,* Mormons had no further legal recourse. They were ground between two millstones, their belief in the plural marriage revelation and their desire to conform to the law of the land. John Taylor, the church president who succeeded Brigham Young, advised polygamist men to hide.

For a decade Mormon husbands went "underground." Many were caught and thrown into prison for a one-year sentence. Federal officials obtained more than a thousand convictions for cohabitation. Mormon wives and children went to look at their husbands and fathers in striped prison garb behind the prison walls. To tighten the vise, Congress raised the ante for continued disobedience. Gradually Mormons were deprived of the rights to vote, to sit on juries, and to hold office. Church property was confiscated. By the end of the decade the church was in danger of losing its temples and other buildings. All but $50,000 of the church's $3,000,000 net worth was in jeopardy.

When Wilford Woodruff became church president after the death of John Taylor in 1887, change seemed necessary. In September 1890, Woodruff informed the Apostles that he had decided plural marriage had to be given up in order to save the church. At a general conference on October 6, 1890, he announced that no further plural marriages would be performed, and the assembled membership raised their hands in acceptance.

Some Mormons thought the announcement was no more than an expedient to relieve pressure from Washington. A people who had defined themselves by their unusual marriage practice could not yield instantly. Faithful Mormons differed on a suitable response; several Apostles, among others, continued to enter into plural marriages. In 1904, President Joseph F. Smith issued a second manifesto to reinforce the first. Although established plural families continued to exist by agreement of all concerned, no new plural marriages were contracted. The era of Mormon polygamy was at an end.

The Manifesto paved the way for Utah's statehood. Statehood put the selection of governing officials in the hands of the Utah population and removed it from the president in Washington. Home rule meant almost as much to Utah Mormons in 1896, when statehood was finally granted, as it did to the Americans who freed themselves from Britain in 1776. But, though freed from federal control, Mormons knew they could not return to the theocracy that the federal government had long opposed. Before statehood was granted, the church dissolved the political party that for decades had stood for pro-Mormon policies, and Mormons distributed themselves between the two national parties. The natural inclination of Mormons was toward the Democratic Party because of its emphasis on states' rights, but in order to win the support of the Republican Party, then dominant in Washington, many church leaders migrated in that direction, and lay members followed in their wake.

The outstanding issues were not settled until the seating of Reed Smoot in the U.S. Senate in 1907. In 1903, the Utah state legislature overwhelmingly chose Smoot, an Apostle but not a polygamist, for the Senate. Because of his high position in the church hierarchy, the Senate challenged his seating on grounds that he represented a church believed to be surreptitiously practicing polygamy and that he was under the thumb of the church president. The Senate investigation that followed became an occasion for the still virulent suspicion of the Mormons to vent itself. The Senate was besieged with petitions against Smoot, invoking all the bad images of Mormonism that had coursed through the anti-Mormon literature for decades.

The church president at the time, Joseph F. Smith, nephew of Joseph Smith, was called to testify and was repeatedly questioned about the continuation of polygamy and even more strenuously about his control of Mormon politics. The old image of theocratic government that had motivated federal government policy for half a century was brought into the open. Was it not true that as president of the church, Joseph F. Smith received revelations? Was it not therefore true that any faithful Mormon was obligated to comply with his revelations? Did it not follow that Reed Smoot would be, therefore, under the control of the church president? Repeated reassurances that Smoot was free to vote his own conscience and that the church president did not dictate policy to Mormon politicians went largely unheard. The logic of revelation seemed to lead inexorably to the dominance of church leaders.

Smoot was finally seated only when President Theodore Roosevelt intervened on his behalf.

The hearings ended, but the question of church control would not die. A century later, when Mitt Romney, the Mormon former governor of Massachusetts, announced his candidacy for the U.S. presidency in 2007, the press assaulted him with the same questions. Was he free to vote his own mind, or was he not? Romney, however, had the century-long record of the Mormon Church in politics on which to rest his case. The church had occasionally taken stands on issues it considered to have moral import such as gambling or Prohibition, but it had not imposed its will on Mormon politicians or the Mormon people. Indeed, against the express wishes of the church president, Utah cast the deciding vote for the repeal of Prohibition in 1932.

Over the years, the church has made its political predilections known to politicians both Mormon and not, but it has not made compliance a condition of membership or of good standing. Having learned its lesson with Reed Smoot at the beginning of the century, the church left Mormon politicians free to vote their own consciences, even when their decisions went contrary to church political positions. The long battle with a hostile Congress had taught the church to give up the theocratic impulse that had roiled its relations with the nation through the nineteenth century.

The ultimate legacy

The impact of late-nineteenth-century history on modern Mormonism is at best ambiguous. Mormons would like to forget much of this past: plural marriage, the conflict with the federal government, Mountain Meadows. That history is not easily absorbed into Mormons' sense of themselves in the twenty-first century. They like to think more about the pioneers, the Brigham Young who directed settlement of a vast intermountain region, the tens of thousands of emigrants who crossed the country and settled in desolate little patches of the American West, and the heroic stories of ancestors who joined the church in their homelands and gave up everything to come to Utah.

The true significance of the nineteenth century in Mormon history is not always visible in the welter of many lives and many conflicts. Rising out of the thousands of individual pioneer accounts is the larger story of the creation of the Mormon people. Every year immigrants poured into Utah from all sections of the United States and from many European nations. They came speaking only Danish, German, or Dutch. They had to slough off much of their previous culture and find a place for themselves among strangers. In their little wards, they became first and foremost Mormons, bonded to the new society by their own sacrifices. Pressures from the government and hostile public opinion succeeded only in welding them all the more inseparably to their faith.

Joseph Smith's vision of Zion guided Brigham Young's plans for these people. Young wanted to create a new culture just as Smith wanted a new society. One of the early buildings erected in Salt Lake City served as a theater. The University of Deseret was organized in 1869, and Brigham Young Academy in 1875. The church founded schools and hospitals. Young was willing to go beyond standard American capitalism to experiment with economic institutions more in keeping with Joseph Smith's Zion. He formed cooperatives and communal economic orders. When he organized a department store to compete with non-Mormon merchants, Young called it Zion's Cooperative Mercantile Institution and inscribed the same words over its door that appeared on the temple: "Holiness to the Lord." His aim was to sacralize every part of life.

Was all this lost in the twentieth century? Much of it was. Young's plans foundered after the government required the church to dismantle the theocracy. The Zion cooperatives were transformed into capitalist enterprises. Most schools were closed or turned over to the state. The church gave up its plans for constructing a complete culture and society. But the ideals could not be completely stamped out. By the time Mormons began to disperse to other parts of the nation in the twentieth century, the migrants, once a disparate conglomerate of many national groups, left Utah as Mormons. They were able to re-create Mormon culture in California, Chicago, and New York. Even without a professional clergy, Mormons formed little wards all over the United States that functioned as effectively as the congregations in the heartland.

After a century of retreat from theocratic society, Mormons today still harbor remnants of Smith's Zion ideals. In the twenty-first century, Mormon artists and writers more than ever incorporate Mormon themes into their work. Mormon journals, Mormon presses, and Mormon scholarly societies have proliferated. Mormons still think of themselves as a people as much as a church. The question is whether the traditional hopes for Zion that were fostered in nineteenth-century Utah can be pursued amidst the democratic pluralism of modern America.

Chapter 7
The Mormon world

Assimilation

The end of polygamy in 1890 and the achievement of Utah statehood in 1896 altered profoundly the relationship between Mormonism and the rest of the United States. For the first time, Mormons could aspire to national respectability. Although suspicion still existed throughout the country, plural marriage no longer stood as an insurmountable barrier to sympathetic understanding of Mormon culture.

Almost immediately the church began to cultivate a new image: happy families, loyal citizens, and industrious workers in contrast to the darker images of Mormons as seditious fanatics, theocrats, and polygamists. In 1902, the church opened a Bureau of Information that over the century burgeoned into an elaborate public affairs program., These agencies told the world about the Mormon people as well as Mormon belief. Visitors to Utah reported favorably on communal cooperation and a simple, wholesome lifestyle. In 1929, the Mormon Tabernacle Choir began broadcasting a weekly performance on national radio from Temple Square, quickly becoming a major public relations asset. Rather than emphasizing doctrine, the church drew attention to Mormon culture and society. Mormonism was not just the true church but a happy people.

**11. The 360-voice Mormon Tabernacle Choir has been broadcasting
Music and the Spoken Word since 1929.**

Mormons hungered for acceptance by the larger American society.
Anxious to be relieved of the infamy that burdened the church
through the nineteenth century, they enthusiastically welcomed
every favorable article in the national press. During wartime,
Mormons emphasized their patriotism by exceeding their quotas
for enlistments in the armed forces. In some ways, Mormons
became super-Americans. Particularly in the 1950s, the Mormon
emphasis on solid families and traditional virtues made them seem
ideal citizens.

At the same time, Mormons were not ready to blend completely
with American society. They were as determined as ever to
maintain their distinctiveness. With polygamy's demise, new
markers came to the fore. In the first half of the twentieth
century, a body of health rules called the Word of Wisdom received
particular emphasis. An 1833 revelation to Joseph Smith had
counseled the saints not to use tobacco, alcohol, or hot drinks,
later interpreted to mean tea and coffee. Through most of the

nineteenth century, these injunctions were referred to in sermons but not strictly enforced. Mild use of alcohol was not uncommon, and British converts continued to drink tea. In the first decades of the twentieth century, the evils of these practices became more evident, especially as a vigorous temperance movement swept the nation, culminating in federal Prohibition in 1920. The church presidents preached more strenuously against the forbidden substances in the Word of Wisdom, and columns in church magazines described the ill effects of tobacco and liquor. By the 1920s, the Word of Wisdom had become a measure of faithfulness. Compliance was required for entrance into the temple. Enforcement of the standards simultaneously differentiated Mormons from the Americans with whom they mingled. At cocktail parties Mormons said "no, thanks."

The diaspora

The elimination of the polygamy barrier coincided with the dispersal of the Mormon population into other parts of the world. By the beginning of the twentieth century, the requirement of gathering to Zion in Utah was relaxed. The best land in the Great Basin had long been taken up, and Mormon pioneers were moving into eastern Oregon, southern Canada, and northern Mexico. Beginning with a trickle before World War I and growing to a flood in the 1920s and 1930s, Mormons migrated to the West Coast and then eastward toward Denver and beyond.

The Great Depression hurried a trend that continued unabated through the twentieth century. Mormons sought their fortunes where they could find the best opportunities. Brigham Young had refused to take the Mormons to California in 1847, knowing the Saints would once again be thrust into communities of gentiles, risking further persecution. But once the gathering to Utah had strengthened their society and culture, Mormons were ready to take on the larger world.

They left the tiny Mormon villages of Utah, Idaho, and Arizona by the thousands and relocated in places like Los Angeles, San Francisco, and Portland, Oregon. Rather than being directed, as were the Saints who settled Utah, they went individually in search of better jobs. The church organized a stake in Los Angeles in 1927 and in San Francisco, Portland, and Seattle soon after. In 1934, a stake was formed in New York City, where Mormons were beginning to migrate for schooling, the arts, and business. The establishment of stakes in the diaspora represented the church's recognition that the Mormon arena was no longer confined to the Great Basin. Zion could be built wherever Mormons lived. After World War II, as global expansion carried Mormons beyond national boundaries, stakes were organized on every continent. Mormonism was becoming a world religion.

The problem of the diaspora was how to prevent assimilation from diluting Mormon identity. In the tiny Mormon villages of the heartland, the bishop knew everyone in town. Everyone was accounted for and ministered to. In large cities, Mormons could drift away. Recognizing the problem, church leaders re-created Mormon villages in the new urban settings, building on programs already developed for Utah cities.

Wards became cultural centers for a host of activities going far beyond standard religious practice. The stakes organized softball and basketball leagues. Wards put on plays, formed choruses, sponsored weekly dances, and planned camping trips. The church held weekly after-school Primary meetings for children under twelve. One evening a week, the young people gathered for classes, Boy Scout meetings, dances, and play rehearsals. The church became the largest institutional sponsor of Scouting in the country. Mature women came to Relief Society weekday afternoons to teach each other the gospel and home crafts. Mormon youth learned to sing harmony and dance the tango, to act and to speak.

An elaborate system for accounting for every individual accompanied the cultural activities. Leaders and teachers kept their eyes on each member, watching for signs of disaffection, intervening to help with problems, offering friendship and counseling. Each month the wards reported their activities to Salt Lake City, especially the percentage of church attendance, the measure of keeping people in the faith. This brave effort to involve everyone now defined Zion. In Missouri and Illinois, Zion had been a city; in Utah, it was a landscape of villages; in the urban diaspora, it was the ward with its extensive programs.

For half a century, the inner work of the church, as contrasted with its outward missionary labors, was to establish these church programs in every ward and stake. Their management required extensive training and vast human resources. Just keeping the youth programs afloat called for the services of dozens of adult men and women. The record-keeping alone was taxing. Worship for Mormons to a large extent consisted of fulfilling one's church calling. One learned to love others, to give of oneself, and to serve God by accepting a calling and giving one's best.

The absence of paid clergy of any kind meant that the congregation as a whole carried the burden of this immensely ambitious program. Besides the activities, ward leaders assigned each adult four or five families to visit and help each month. The men went out in pairs as ward (later home) teachers and the women as visiting teachers. Each family, whether active or inactive, received a visit. The teachers offered help where it was needed and gave a little gospel lesson.

By the last third of the century, this system of mutual service was straining church members' capacities. Many members, especially those new to the church, faltered under the demands. The gasoline shortage of the 1970s provided an occasion for cutting back. In the name of conserving fuel, church leaders compressed the meeting schedule and reduced the range of activities. Instead of meeting both morning and afternoon on Sundays—sometimes necessitating families drive a half hour or more each way twice a day—and holding meetings for each age group on weekdays, the church shifted to one three-hour block on Sundays and terminated most of the weekday meetings. Now Mormons meet for a "sacrament meeting" of seventy minutes, followed by a Sunday School class to study the scriptures. Then the men gather in priesthood meeting and the women in Relief Society while the children and youth meet in their own classes.

While cutbacks were occurring in most programs, the church put even stronger emphasis on religious classes, called seminary, for young people of high school age. In most areas of the church, Latter-day Saint high schoolers rise early in the morning and travel to a church building or a home for a forty-five-minute lesson on the scriptures before they go to school. In areas of higher Mormon density, the schools release students for one period a day to cross the street to a seminary building where paid instructors teach the gospel. The special attention given to teenagers shows the church's concern about its youth at the age when they begin to make their own decisions about what they will be in their lives.

The family

The reduction of church programs—save for seminary—reflected a new direction for the church in the diaspora. Instead of enveloping individuals in programs to keep them in the faith, church leaders emphasized the family. The responsibility for rearing young Mormons, they now taught, lies primarily with parents rather than with the official church. Too many meetings divided families by taking children and parents out of the home to participate in or staff church programs. With the reduced church load, parents would have time and energy to teach their children themselves. A new emphasis was given to weekly "family home evenings," in which parents instruct their children and the family can air its problems. Monday evening was reserved for these, a night free of all other church meetings. Families were to gather for lessons and fun: games, refreshments, singing, and talk.

The current Mormon emphasis on family partially grew out of the challenges of the diaspora, but it was grounded in the doctrine of eternal marriage going back to Joseph Smith. Smith's revelations promised that families sealed by the priesthood in the temple would continue into eternity. Children born to parents already sealed in the temple are automatically sealed to their parents. If their parents were married civilly, the children are to be sealed in a temple ceremony. They kneel in white clothes at an altar and place their hands on the hands of their parents and siblings while the ceremony is pronounced, signifying that all the members are bound to one another for eternity. In the second half of the twentieth century, protecting these families became a major goal of church programs.

12. The church urges families to hold "family home evening" every Monday night for instruction, counseling, and fun.

Mormons are deeply concerned about the debilitating influences of societal moral decline on their children. As long as Mormons were sequestered in their little villages, it was relatively easy to keep the evils of the world at bay. Mixed in with the larger American population, however, Mormon children are at risk along with everyone else. The church has taken strong stands against pornography and gambling. Church leaders came out openly against the Equal Rights Amendment for women on the grounds that women's roles were being redefined in ways that reduced the importance of mothering. Church leaders have opposed legalizing gay marriage out of fear that traditional marriage will be weakened.

In general the church has come down with conservative Christians on most outstanding social issues, including abortion, though Mormon policy takes account of the woman's well-being more than the most rigid anti-abortionists do. Most Mormons see these political positions as one with the defense of sexual chastity and marital fidelity. They want to defend the family against every corrosive force at work in the modern world.

A formal statement from the church presidency issued in 1995 and called "The Family: A Proclamation to the World" reemphasized traditional roles for husbands and wives. Husbands are to provide for the family and wives to nurture the children. The proclamation could be read as a reaffirmation of patriarchy, but in practice male domination is discouraged. The proclamation states that both parents are to rear the children in "love and righteousness." Although Mormons still speak of the man as head of the household, the church manual on family relations emphasizes partnership. When crying children have to be taken out of a church meeting, the husband steps out as often as the wife.

Blacks and the priesthood

After World War II, the church flourished in an ever-growing number of countries, particularly in Latin America and the

Philippines. Missionaries reported more requests for teaching than they could accommodate; missionary pairs sometimes baptized dozens of converts each month. Stakes and wards could scarcely be organized fast enough to meet the need. Mormonism seemed on its way to becoming a global religion.

Despite this success, the church confronted a barrier of its own making: its historical exclusion of black males from the priesthood. The origins of this doctrine are not altogether clear. Passages in Joseph Smith's translations indicate that a lineage associated with Ham and the Egyptian pharaohs was forbidden the priesthood. Connecting the ancient pharaohs with modern Africans and African Americans required a speculative leap, but by the time of Brigham Young, the leap was made. Joseph Smith had approved the ordination of a few black people, taken a strong stand against slavery, and favored equal opportunities for all Americans, but Brigham Young announced a ban on ordaining blacks. From the 1850s on, black people were not ordained to the priesthood as a matter of principle.

In the nineteenth century, this practice caused little conflict or remorse, but as the twentieth century went on, the exclusion of blacks seemed increasingly unfair and unjustified. During the civil rights movement of the 1960s, both Mormon and non-Mormon activists brought intense pressure against the church to change the practice. Athletic teams refused to play with teams from Brigham Young University. Disillusioned Mormons withdrew from church participation. For some Mormons, the issue of black men and the priesthood was a major moral crisis.

Change came not as a result of pressures within the United States, however, but from the church's own missionary program. The practice of priesthood exclusion complicated proselytizing among black populations in places like Brazil. Converts of mixed ancestry, common in Brazil, faced baffling questions. Were they black or not? How could they determine the presence of an African strain in their ancestry? Members of dark complexion found themselves in a limbo of uncertainty. With a large population of mixed-race Mormons, construction of a temple, the final step in bringing the full church program to a nation, was problematic. Who would man it? Who would be admitted?

Church leaders had long said the time would come when the ban on black priesthood holding would be lifted, though a time frame was never specified. All that was certain was that a revelation was required. Church presidents from midcentury on had concerned themselves with the issue and sought guidance. Finally, in 1978, President Spencer W. Kimball announced that the time had come to change the policy, and the Lord had confirmed the decision. The announcement was greeted with joy and relief among the Mormon population, who had been burdened with a disquieting practice. The priesthood was immediately conferred on black converts who had patiently borne the pain of exclusion for many years and now felt their faith was vindicated.

Mormonism and modernism

The removal of the ban on black priesthood members brought the church more in step with modern sensibilities and eased assimilation into contemporary life, but the largest obstacle to assimilation could never be surmounted: the claim that miraculous events underlay the founding of Mormonism. What was a modern, educated citizen in an advanced capitalist nation to make of Joseph Smith's story of an angel, gold plates, and inspired translation? How could the visions and visitations be considered anything more than psychological illusions?

There was no room in the modern worldview for angels. The Yale literary critic Harold Bloom has said that Joseph Smith's angels once would have been considered perfectly natural, but since the Enlightenment angels have been contrary to the laws of nature. The Roman Catholic sociologist Thomas O'Dea, whose book on

Mormonism is considered one of the most astute commentaries by an outside observer, predicted that the Mormon emphasis on education was on a collision course with fundamental Mormon beliefs. As the Mormon population learned the critical methods of scientific scholarship, their own core beliefs would be doomed.

Over the past century, the church has suffered the loss of many of its educated members, but probably no more than the seepage of believers at every level of education. Studies of church activity show that PhD-holding members are more likely to be fully engaged than high school graduates. Mormons feel that their founding miracles are no more unlikely than the other founding miracles of Christianity. All the revealed religions of the world begin with divine intervention in human life. Christianity has the Incarnation and the Resurrection, Judaism its God at Sinai and the deliverance of Israel from Egypt, Islam the conveyance of God's word in the Qur'an. These miracles remain controversial centuries after they are purported to have occurred. Critics attribute them to illusion or legend; believers hold on to them as signs of God's involvement in human affairs.

The debate over the rationality of the miracles—though carried on passionately—is not quite on point for Mormon believers. Their miracles represent an attitude toward the world. Miracles imply that God takes an interest in humans. If some educated Mormons drift away, overwhelmed by the dissonance with modernity, other young Mormons keep the faith and delight in their independence. Being outliers on the intellectual landscape empowers young Mormon intellectuals to challenge and go beyond the conventional assumptions of modern scholarly disciplines and find a way of their own.

This loyalty to Mormonism baffles outside observers. How can informed Mormons remain true to a religion based on miracles, behind the times in its adherence to conservative social principles, and subject to the authoritarian control of the church hierarchy? Mormonism appears to be the quintessence of anti-modernism. How can it survive?

The most common explanation is Mormon communalism. Mormons create congregational communities in which everyone has a place. Even skeptical members are reluctant to break the ties, feeling at home in a society where everyone watches out for one another temporally and spiritually. The Mormon congregation is a beehive where everyone is involved. The wealthy and powerful do not stand aside but become the bishops and high councilors, the scoutmasters and youth leaders. No one is exempt; no one is excluded. Those tight social bonds weave individuals into a powerful structure many cannot bear to leave.

Mormonism, moreover, offers people a way of life. It provides a basic personal discipline for modern living. Its Word of Wisdom and insistence on chastity offer a foundation for a clean life. Mormon young people live in a world where abstinence of all kinds is the rule, not the exception. They grow up knowing it is wrong to smoke and drink. Adults conform to the same rules. Young people may stray from the discipline or even flaunt its strictures to prove their independence, but they feel the power of a community with standards. Converts sometimes come into the church just to give their children a place in that world. It is a good that even jaundiced Mormons value.

Beyond the community and the wholesome life, Mormonism gives its members a place in the universe. The stories of eternity laid out in Joseph Smith's revelations imply a basic attitude toward existence. Mormons imagine the beginnings when they stood before God and were offered the chance to come to earth, gain a body, and be tested. Here they are passing through another test to see if they will remain faithful to God amid adversity and temptation.

This simple story, much of it found in the Bible but accentuated and enlarged in Joseph Smith's writings, is basically optimistic. The story begins with a God striving to save his children, and in the end he brings all but a few of them into a kingdom of glory. Mormons feel a strong obligation to go along with God, to make the most of their time on earth, to acquire intelligence and knowledge, and to help everyone else along the same path. It is an activist attitude. Salvation requires exertion and constructive effort. Mormons feel they are building the kingdom of God on earth in anticipation of the time when it will be joined with the kingdom of heaven. The same activist stance carries over to the next life, which they envision as an extension of what happens here. People minister to one another, they organize, they establish kingdoms where growing souls can learn godliness. Even borderline Mormons feel the strength of that story.

All of this is in the background at the weekly services in the chapel. Ordinary Mormon services are low church in the extreme. The bishop stands up and makes announcements before beginning the meeting. The Sacrament is blessed by young men sixteen or seventeen years old and passed to everyone in the meeting by boys twelve and thirteen. Members of the congregation take turns speaking, often as couples. They tell how the Lord has helped them and give little messages about faith or Christ or reading the scriptures. They speak colloquially. They tell simple stories. All the while children chirp and cry in the congregation and have to be taken out of the meeting. Everyone at every level is involved. Young people present five-minute messages to prepare them for more elaborate speaking assignments later. In Primary, children four and five give brief talks. The meetings are invariably inclusive—and not always stimulating. But members listen patiently, knowing their turn may come next.

Mormons often have trouble explaining what they believe. They usually say something about the return of revelation and priesthood. Often they will refer to their own experience with personal revelation. That is probably as good an answer as any, but it falls short of the actual nature of Mormon faith. Mormonism is an array of doctrines, communal interaction, ritual, private worship, and spiritual history integrated into a life experience. The complexity and comprehensiveness of the whole are the reason Mormons keep their faith. They know they are part of a satisfying and enriching culture. To depart from the Mormon circle is to abandon a plenteous and ordered existence for the perplexities and sorrows of modern life. All this gives Mormons reason to hold on to the faith at the center of their lives.

Appendix

Articles of Faith

In 1842, John Wentworth, editor of the Chicago Democrat, *asked Joseph Smith for a sketch of the rise of the Latter-day Saints for George Barstow, who was writing a history of New Hampshire, where Wentworth was born. Barstow did not publish Smith's essay, but a brief summation of beliefs at its conclusion was added to Latter-day Saints scripture in 1880 under the title of "Articles of Faith."*

1. We believe in God, the Eternal Father, and in His Son, Jesus Christ, and in the Holy Ghost.

2. We believe that men will be punished for their own sins, and not for Adam's transgression.

3. We believe that through the Atonement of Christ, all mankind may be saved, by obedience to the laws and ordinances of the Gospel.

4. We believe that the first principles and ordinances of the Gospel are: first, Faith in the Lord Jesus Christ; second, Repentance; third, Baptism by immersion for the remission of sins; fourth, Laying on of hands for the gift of the Holy Ghost.

5. We believe that a man must be called of God, by prophecy, and by the laying on of hands by those who are in authority, to preach the Gospel and administer in the ordinances thereof.

6. We believe in the same organization that existed in the Primitive Church, namely, apostles, prophets, pastors, teachers, evangelists, and so forth.

7. We believe in the gift of tongues, prophecy, revelation, visions, healing, interpretation of tongues, and so forth.

8. We believe the Bible to be the word of God as far as it is translated correctly; we also believe the Book of Mormon to be the word of God.

9. We believe all that God has revealed, all that He does now reveal, and we believe that He will yet reveal many great and important things pertaining to the Kingdom of God.

10. We believe in the literal gathering of Israel and in the restoration of the Ten Tribes; that Zion (the New Jerusalem) will be built upon the American continent; that Christ will reign personally upon the earth; and, that the earth will be renewed and receive its paradisiacal glory.

11. We claim the privilege of worshiping Almighty God according to the dictates of our own conscience, and allow all men the same privilege, let them worship how, where, or what they may.

12. We believe in being subject to kings, presidents, rulers, and magistrates, in obeying, honoring, and sustaining the law.

13. We believe in being honest, true, chaste, benevolent, virtuous, and in doing good to all men; indeed, we may say that we follow the admonition of Paul. We believe all things, we hope all things, we have endured many things, and hope to be able to endure all things. If there is anything virtuous, lovely, or of good report or praiseworthy, we seek after these things.

Articles of Faith, *The Pearl of Great Price* (Salt Lake City: Church of Jesus Christ of Latter-day Saints, 1981).

Notes

Chapter 1

1. Joseph Smith, "History, 1832," Dean C. Jessee, ed. *The Personal Writings of Joseph Smith*, rev. ed. (Salt Lake City: Deseret Book, 2002), 9.
2. "Alexander Neibaur Report, 1844," Dean C. Jessee, ed., *The Papers of Joseph Smith* (Salt Lake City: Deseret Book, 1989), 1:461.

Chapter 2

1. Joseph Smith, "History, 1832," Dean C. Jessee, ed. *The Personal Writings of Joseph Smith*, rev. ed. (Salt Lake City: Desert Book, 2002), 11.
2. Ibid.
3. William D. Purple, "Reminiscences" (1877), in Dan Vogel, ed., *Early Mormon Documents*, 5 vols. (Salt Lake City: Signature Books, 1996–2003), 4:135.
4. Emma Smith Bidamon, "Interview with Joseph Smith III, February 1879," in Vogel, ed., *Early Mormon Documents*, 1:539.
5. Vogel, ed., *Early Mormon Documents*, 1:542.

Chapter 3

1. Thomas F. O'Dea, *The Mormons* (Chicago: University of Chicago Press, 1957), 116.
2. *Missouri Intelligencer* (Columbia), August 10, 1833.

Chapter 5

1. Joseph Smith Jr. *The Words of Joseph Smith: The Contemporary Accounts of the Nauvoo Discourses of the Prophet Joseph,* ed. Andrew F. Ehat and Lyndon W. Cook (Provo, Utah: Religious Studies Center, Brigham Young University, 1980), 360.
2. Ibid., 346.
3. Ibid., 360, 346.

Further reading

General histories and interpretations

Allen, James B., and Glen M. Leonard. *The Story of the Latter-day Saints.* 2nd ed., rev. and enl. Salt Lake City: Deseret Book, 1992.

Arrington, Leonard, and Davis Bitton. *The Mormon Experience.* New York: Knopf, 1979.

Bushman, Richard Lyman, and Claudia L. Bushman. *Building the Kingdom of God.* New York: Oxford University Press, 2001.

Mauss, Armand L. *The Angel and the Beehive: The Mormon Struggle with Assimilation.* Urbana: University of Illinois Press, 1994.

O'Dea, Thomas. *The Mormons.* Chicago: University of Chicago Press, 1957.

Shipps, Jan. *Mormonism: The Story of a New Religious Tradition.* Urbana: University of Illinois Press, 1985.

Joseph Smith

Brodie, Fawn. *No Man Knows My History: The Life of Joseph Smith the Mormon Prophet.* New York: Knopf, 1945.

Bushman, Richard Lyman. *Joseph Smith: Rough Stone Rolling.* New York: Knopf, 2005.

Vogel, Dan. *Joseph Smith: The Making of a Prophet.* Salt Lake City: Signature Books, 2004.

Book of Mormon

Givens, Terryl L. *By the Hand of Mormon: The American Scripture That Launched a New World Religion.* New York: Oxford University Press, 2002.

Metcalfe, Brent Lee. *New Approaches to the Book of Mormon: Explorations in Critical Methodology*. Salt Lake City: Signature Books, 1993.

Nibley, Hugh. *Since Cumorah*. 1967; rpt., Salt Lake City: Deseret Book and FARMS, 1988.

Sorensen, John L. *An Ancient American Setting for the Book of Mormon*. Salt Lake City: Deseret Book and FARMS, 1996.

Founding period

Allen, James B., Ronald K. Esplin, and David J. Whittaker. *Men with a Mission: The Quorum of the Twelve Apostles in the British Isles*. Salt Lake City: Deseret Book, 1992.

Backman, Milton V. *The Heavens Resound: A History of the Latter-day Saints in Ohio, 1830–1838*. Salt Lake City: Deseret Book, 1983.

Flanders, Robert B. *Nauvoo: Kingdom on the Mississippi*. Urbana: University of Illinois Press, 1965.

Leonard, Glen M. *Nauvoo: A Place of Peace, a People of Promise*. Salt Lake City: Deseret Book, 2001.

LeSueur, Stephen C. *The 1838 Mormon War in Missouri*. Columbia: University of Missouri Press, 1987.

Newell, Linda King, and Val Tippetts Avery. *Mormon Enigma: Emma Smith, Prophet's Wife, "Elect Lady," Polygamy's Foe, 1804–1879*. 2nd ed. Urbana: University of Illinois Press, 1994.

Underwood, Grant. *The Millenarian World of Early Mormonism*. Urbana: University of Illinois Press, 1993.

Nineteenth-century Utah

Arrington, Leonard. *Brigham Young: American Moses*. New York: Knopf, 1985.

——— . *Great Basin Kingdom: Economic History of the Latter-day Saints, 1830–1890*. Cambridge: Harvard University Press, 1958.

Bigler, David. *Forgotten Kingdom: The Mormon Theocracy in the American West, 1847–1896*. Logan: University of Utah Press, 1998.

Bitton, Davis. *George Q. Cannon*. Salt Lake City: Deseret Book, 1999.

Givens, Terryl. *People of Paradox: A History of Mormon Culture*. New York: Oxford University Press, 2007.

Walker, Ronald W. *Wayward Saints: The Godbeites and Brigham Young*. Urbana: University of Illinois Press, 1998.

Plural marriage

Compton, Todd M. *In Sacred Loneliness: The Plural Wives of Joseph Smith*. Salt Lake City: Signature Books, 1997.

Daynes, Katherine. *More Wives than One: Transformation of the Mormon Marriage System, 1840–1910*. Urbana: University of Illinois Press, 2001.

Gordon, Sarah Barringer. *The Mormon Question: Polygamy and Constitutional Conflict in the Nineteenth Century*. Chapel Hill: University of North Carolina Press, 2002.

Van Wagoner, Richard S. *Mormon Polygamy: A History*. 3rd ed. Salt Lake City: Signature Books, 1992.

Twentieth-century Mormonism

Alexander, Thomas. *Mormonism in Transition, 1890–1930: A History of the Latter-day Saints*. Urbana: University of Illinois Press, 1986.

Cornwall, Marie, Tim B. Heaton, and Lawrence A. Young, eds. *Contemporary Mormonism: Social Science Perspectives*. Urbana: University of Illinois Press, 1994.

Prince, Gregory A., and William Robert Wright. *David O. McKay and the Rise of Modern Mormonism*. Salt Lake City: University of Utah Press, 2005.

Theology

Barlow, Philip. *Mormons and the Bible: The Place of the Latter-day Saints in American Religion*. New York: Oxford University Press, 1991.

Davies, Douglas. *The Mormon Culture of Salvation: Force, Grace, and Glory*. Aldershot, Eng.: Ashgate, 2000.

McMurrin, Sterling. *The Theological Foundations of the Mormon Religion*. Salt Lake City: University of Utah Press, 1959.

Talmage, James E. *The Articles of Faith*. Salt Lake City: Deseret News, 1899.

Race

Mauss, Armand L. *All Abraham's Children: Changing Mormon Conceptions of Race and Lineage*. Urbana: University of Illinois Press, 2003.

Web sites

Official Web sites

The Church of Jesus Christ of Latter-day Saints
www.lds.org
The site is designed for church members looking for help with
talks and lessons and for nonmembers wanting general
information. Offers access to a large online library of church
magazines and books plus current news of church events. A tab for
newspeople leads to basic information on church history and
doctrine.

The Church of Jesus Christ of Latter-day Saints
www.mormon.org
The place for non-Mormons to go for information about doctrines
and practices. Offers simple, straightforward answers to basic
questions, including some tough ones.

Family Search
www.familysearch.org
A large proportion of the genealogical records in the church archives
are available at this site. These are not, however, original sources,
but information that has been submitted by genealogists. The church
has not edited or checked the records' accuracy. Good for genealogical
leads, but the information should be confirmed in the sources.

Community of Christ
www.cofchrist.org
This single site for the Community of Christ serves both members
and nonmembers. Offers help to ministers as well as information on
church events, study guides, and summaries of basic church beliefs.

Mormon intellectuals

Times and Seasons
www.timesandseasons.org
A blog with regular and invited authors and responses from
anyone who is interested. Basically attracts faithful Mormons but
ones with many, many questions.

By Common Consent
www.bycommonconsent.com
Like the above, this blog is sometimes irreverent but basically
faithful. Also offers links to breaking LDS news.

Foundation for Apologetic Information and Research (FAIR)
www.fairlds.org
An independent organization that tries to answer every criticism of
Mormonism and present scholarly defenses of Mormon claims.

Helpful services

LDS Today
www.ldstoday.com
Compiles the latest news of the Church of Jesus Christ of Latter-
day Saints from all sources. Run by a private person.

Mormon Archipelago
www.ldsblogs.org
Lists the addresses of more than sixty Mormon blogs with latest
headlines from an assortment of them.

Index

plural marriage in, 86–87; Relief Society in, 93; tolerance in, 43

New Jerusalem, 36, 45, 68

New York City, 106; temple in, 58

O

O'Dea, Thomas F., 35, 112–13

Oregon, 105

P

Palmyra, New York, 9

Pearl of Great Price, 68, 71

Perpetual Education Fund, 41–42

Peter (the apostle), 5, 50

persecution, 10–12, 13, 42–44

plural marriage, 86–91; and fundamentalists, 14; Joseph Smith institutes, 2, 11, 86–88; opposition to, 92, 97–99; renounced, 2–3, 89

polygamy. *See* plural marriage

Portland, Oregon, 106

Presbyterian Church, 9

priesthood: Aaronic, 49–50, 53, 62; and black people, 110–12; democratic aspects of, 51–54; and exclusivity, 60–62; and gender, 14; Melchizedek, 50–51, 53, 62; restoration of, 49–51

Q

Qur'an, 26, 113

R

Relief Society, 93–94

Reorganized Church of Jesus Christ of Latter Day Saints: membership, 1; modernizes, 14; organized, 14, 83–84

restoration, 1; as definition of Mormonism, 4–6; as missionary message, 46

revelation: members receive, 26–31, 54; ongoing, 3, 18–19, 26–27; in restoration, 5

Rigdon, Sidney, 81–82

Roman Catholicism, 4, 43; and priesthood, 49–51

Romney, Mitt, 100

S

sacrament of the Lord's Supper, 53, 115

Salt Lake City: church headquarters, 1, 13–14, 84; temple in, 57–58; theater in, 101

San Francisco, California, 106

Seattle, Washington, 106

Second Great Awakening, 9

seminary, 108

Sharon, Vermont, 9

Smith, Asael, 9

Smith, Emma: joins RLDS, 83; marriage, 20; and plural marriage, 86–87; and translation, 20, 22–24

Smith, Joseph F., 98–99

Smith, Joseph Jr., xii; assassinated, 2, 13, 96; and black people, 111; and Book of Abraham, 69–71; and Book of Mormon, 19–24; and Book of Moses, 64–67; cosmological thought of, 71–74; democratizes revelation, 27; democratizes authority, 51–55; doctrine of God, 6–7, 71–74; doctrine of heaven, 75–76; early life, 9; and economic equality, 38–39; family doctrines of, 109–10; First Vision of, 16–19; history of, 8–13; jailed, 11; and magic, 21–22; organizes church, 1, 9–10, 24; organizes councils, 52–53; place of, in Mormonism, 8; and plural marriage, 86–88; and priesthood, 49–51; as restorer,